Good Things from Nantucket's North Shore

A Culinary Memoir

Frances Ruley Karttunen

Also by Frances Ruley Karttunen

Between Worlds: Interpreters, Guides, and Survivors

The Other Islanders: People Who Pulled Nantucket's Oars

Law and Disorder in Old Nantucket

Nantucket Places and People 1: Main Street to the North Shore

Nantucket Places and People 2: South of Main Street

Nantucket Places and People 3: Out of Town

Nantucket Places and People 4: Underground

Good Things from Nantucket's North Shore: A Culinary Memoir
© 2011 by Frances Ruley Karttunen. All rights reserved.

Printed in the U.S.A. by CreateSpace Publishing
North Charleston, South Carolina

Karttunen, Frances Ruley
fkarttunen.com

Library of Congress Control Number: 2011901045

ISBN-13 978-1456549381

ISBN-10 1456549383

1. Nantucket. 2. History. 3. Food. 4. Memoir.

Front-cover photo: *Autumn harvest at Pine Grove Farm, 1880s.* Nantucket Historical Association.

IN MEMORY OF

my mother,

    Charlotte Gibbs Ruley

her sister,

    Esther Ulrika Gibbs

and their mother,

    Hilda Sofia Österberg Gibbs

And in memory of

    Ellen Ramsdell,

Aunt Esther's companion

in decades of global culinary adventures.

Table of Contents

By Way of a Preface

This is from a collection of nineteenth-century recipes I inherited. Many of the recipes are either labeled "Old Nantucket Recipe" or are attributed to someone born in the 1800s — women such as "Miss Winslow" and "Dr. Folger's Mother." Who the originator of this pie recipe was we will never know.

ORIGINAL

1 1/2 cups cooked pumpkin or squash
1 1/4 cup top milk
3/4 cup granulated sugar
2 eggs
1 teaspoon vanilla
1 teaspoon cinnamon
1/2 teaspoon salt

Beat eggs slightly and add to pumpkin or squash. Add 1cup milk, sugar, and seasonings. Pour into uncooked pastry and gently pour 1/4 cup milk over top of pie. The milk doesn't mix with the filling but remains on top, and the pie has a deep brown, burnished look that is mighty appetizing.

Typically, the recipe as written doesn't mention the size of the pie plate, oven temperature, or baking time. "Top milk" harks back to the days before milk was homogenized, when the cream separated and rose to the top. Only two flavorings are called for, vanilla and cinnamon. In the 1800s they and the sugar would have been luxury enough. The pumpkin or squash would have been fresh, of course, making this pie an autumn harvest treat.

Most of the old Nantucket recipes in the collection do not work well (or at all) with modern ingredients. It takes experimentation to produce something like what was originally intended. I made this pie four times before I managed to produce the burnished deep brown top. All four were tasty, but the first three were unsightly. Here is what led to success.

Preheat the oven to 325°. Prepare a bottom crust in a ten-inch Pyrex or stoneware pie plate.

If you don't have time to make the pie from fresh pumpkin or squash, canned pumpkin will do.

In place of top milk, use evaporated milk or light cream. The evaporated milk produces a firmer filling, while the cream makes a richer-tasting one.

For the burnished top, use whole milk, because cream and evaporated milk are too thick to spread well. Dribble the milk over the filling and then use a pastry brush to gently spread it evenly.

Bake for ninety minutes. At this point the top will have the burnished effect.

Insert a knife into the filling. If it comes away clean, the pie is done.

Cool thoroughly before serving.

Acknowledgments

2010–11 has been the year of the Nantucket memoir. In the spring I read the manuscript of *Nantucket After Boyhood* by Francis Pease, a sequel to his lovely childhood memoir, *My Nantucket Boyhood*. In the fall the Nantucket Atheneum organized a memoir-writing project with the goal of producing a volume of short pieces by many Nantucket residents. I caught the fever, and the result is this little book.

I am doubly in debt to Allen Reinhard for sharing his enthusiasm for the Atheneum project and also for his photograph of the Calder family monument in New North Cemetery that appears in Chapter 12.

My Nantucket cousins and Elvy Perry, one of our Rhode Island cousins, have kindly helped by confirming and augmenting things I recall from childhood.

I am also grateful to Fritz and Anne Schwaller for having given me, nearly two decades ago, a first edition of their own culinary memoir, *Vaguely Hispanic: A Cookbook*, and then, in the summer of 2010, presenting me with a copy of the third edition. Thanks to them, I have vicariously experienced Spain, a country I have visited only twice and all too briefly. I especially treasure their description of summer days in Seville when "it is just too hot to eat, much less chew or cook" — the afternoon heat reducing people to lying on cool tile floors and sipping chilled gazpacho straight from the refrigerator. *Vaguely Hispanic* has been a model for this effort of mine.

Many of the family photographs throughout the chapters were preserved and passed on to me by Cousin Ellen Gibbs Holdgate and

Aunt Esther Gibbs. The 1953 photo of the North Shore Restaurant is by Hollis Burton Engley, and the 1956 photo of my father in Chapter 5 is by George M. Cushing Jr. Those in Chapter 8 of Ellen Ramsdell riding her bicycle, the Sylvaro homestead at 67 North Centre, and Lizzie Sylvaro Ramsdell are all from a collection generously made available to the NHA by Geraldine "G.G." Salisbury. The University of Texas classroom photo in Chapter 10 is by Bertie Acker. The photos in Chapter 11 are from the Boston University Center for Digital Imaging Arts in Waltham, MA. Allen Reinhard took the photo of the Calder family monument in New North Cemetery for Chapter 12, and I heartily thank our next-door friends and neighbors Jean Heron and Gerry Connick for contributing their photo and their bread recipe for that chapter. Other photos are from the magnificent historic image database of the Nantucket Historical Association, which I never tire of exploring.

As ever, I am in debt to Elizabeth Oldham for her editorial guidance, to Ralph Henke for timely and cheerful help in making images available for this volume, to Kenneth Turner Blackshaw for design, and to Helen-Jo Hewitt and Karen Borchert for reading the final product.

Most boundless of all is my gratitude to the homefolks who first taught me about good food: my mother and her sister; my grandmother and her sisters; my big brother Bob and his wife Mary Lou; and Reginald Haskell, my first employer, who taught me almost everything I know to this day about food prep. We all lived within a mile of one another.

Introduction

This book is a happy marriage of memories of good food from my neighborhood and vignettes of the people who have lived and cooked here.

My family has been food-oriented for generations, and as long as I can remember, I have read cookbooks with the same avidity as mystery novels. What's going on here? How will this turn out?

In 1993 I inherited two boxes of recipe cards, the legacy of Aunt Esther Gibbs and Miss Ellen Ramsdell. Three decades earlier, Esther and Ellen had combined their households in what had been Ellen's grandparents' home. Likewise, the recipes in the two boxes were an intermingling of their recipes together with a collection of nineteenth-century Nantucket recipes.

My first thought was to produce a little "benefit" cookbook. Then, in 1996, I was invited to contribute an article about Aunt Esther's restaurant, the North Shore, to the *Radcliffe Culinary Times*, and this inspired me to think of something a little grander.

As I became familiar with the wealth of old photographs in the Nantucket Historical Association's image archive, an even grander concept took shape: an illustrated neighborhood history with a recipe or two at the end of each chapter.

Which of the recipes to choose? The more I thought of the many family members, friends, and neighbors who taught me about good food, the more I wanted to share. Would the prospective neighborhood history have a big appendix with recipes other than those from the boxes I had inherited?

Between 2007 and 2010 I produced five books of essays with bright-colored covers: red, yellow, green, blue, and purple. I was one cover short of a rainbow. Here was a solution. Instead of an appendix to the neighborhood history, the multitude of family recipes could gather in a separate volume with a pumpkin-orange cover.

As for the title I originally had in mind, *Good Things from Nantucket's North Shore: A Neighborhood History with Recipes*, it could bifurcate as well. In the future, look for *Nantucket's North Shore: A Neighborhood History*. That's where I will pair some old Nantucket recipes with many historic photographs.

In the meantime, here are some memories punctuated with food descriptions and recipes from my own lifetime. This is not a conventional cookbook, and readers may be frustrated by my sometimes vague and impressionistic approach to food preparation. In my own defense, this is the way I learned to cook, being encouraged to experiment and to get the feel of what I am doing rather than following step-by-step directions with precise measurements. As an aid, I have compiled two indices, a "culinary index" of foods mentioned, whether in recipes or in discourse, and a second index of the recipes themselves.

The recipes I include here will work with modern, available ingredients. In my experience, as well as in the experience of Esther and Ellen, they are keepers.

This memoir not only omits some measurements and oven temperatures, it also leaves out some of my family members and friends for the reason that we didn't share culinary adventures. There are no contributions, for instance, from my brother Tony and my boy cousins Maurice, Richard, and Donald Gibbs—guys who did not work in restaurants and in my experience didn't engage in food talk. Brother Bob is in the book, thanks to a fine recipe he devised and shared with me.

Maurice Edward Gibbs (1868–1922)

Chapter 1
Grampa Gibbs

I never knew my grandfather, Surfman Maurice Edward Gibbs. He died in the Marine Hospital at Vineyard Haven of injuries sustained while on duty at Madaket Life-Saving Station twenty years before I was born.

He had served many years — first in the United States Life-Saving Service and then in the United States Coast Guard from its inception in 1915 to the end of his life. At age fifty-three and close to retirement, he was still part of a crew that launched heavy wooden lifeboats into the South Shore surf no matter what the conditions. The weekly round of drills went on relentlessly, regardless of weather, the service motto being "You have to go out. You don't have to come back."

According to his obituary, published in the *Inquirer and Mirror*, Maurice Gibbs was "of a genial temperament," "a pleasant companion" to his fellow surfmen, "thorough and efficient, faithful to duty whether ashore or in the surf-boat." He had been a member of Nantucket's Union Lodge and also of the Improved Order of Odd Fellows, and the newspaper concluded that, "As a citizen, he was all a man should be."

With Masonic rites, his body was taken from his house at 12 Cliff Road to interment in the family plot in New North Cemetery.

His untimely death devastated his four children, especially his youngest, my aunt Esther, who was eleven years old when she lost her father. He left his wife a widow for forty years to come, through the Great Depression and World War II, always working to keep their family afloat in an island economy that offered meager rewards. It is said that his pension and death benefit were slow in coming.

12 Cliff Road in the 1890s.
The horse-car tracks at the right lead to the Sea Cliff Inn, built in 1886, for which the name of the street was changed from North Street to Cliff Road.

Despite the challenges, his survivors kept the house—in the family since his great-grandfather, Captain Hezekiah Pinkham, bought it in 1809—with all its accumulation of family papers and artifacts, preserving the memory of Maurice Gibbs as much through recitation of his Nantucket genealogy as through stories about the man himself.

There was one joke that was told again and again. Grampa Gibbs had done the cooking for the Life-Saving Station crew, baking pies by the dozen to satisfy their hearty appetites. The story was that he had pie stamps, but only two. One stamp was M for Mince, and the other was TM for 'T'aint mince.

The history of sea cooks is a long one. They kept Nantucket whalers' crews alive for years on end with meals of salt meat, turtle, hardtack, and—on festive occasions—a steamed pudding known as plum duff. In *Moby-Dick,* Herman Melville, who sailed on a Nantucket whaleship, spends most of a chapter on the merciless teasing of Old Fleece, the *Pequod's* elderly cook, over the proper preparation of a whale steak.

Cooking for land-based life-saving crews allowed much more latitude and refinement, but where had Maurice Gibbs learned his art?

He had grown up almost an orphan, his mother having died of "galloping consumption," as the family story goes, when he was a toddler. His father, Edward Coleman Gibbs, had a taste for putting distance between himself and Nantucket. As a young man he had joined the Gold Rush to California, and after his marriage to Maurice's mother, he took off again, making a second marriage in Illinois, of which his Nantucket family remained unaware, so attenuated was their contact. Edward Gibbs returned to Nantucket only after the deaths of his second wife and his Nantucket mother-in-law and after his son's own marriage. The *Inquirer and Mirror* reported on July 22, 1905, that, "Edward C. Gibbs, after many years residence in Illinois, has returned to his old home in Nantucket to spend the remainder of his days with his son Maurice E. Gibbs." Maurice's family cared for the old man to the end of his days, and in 1913 buried him next to his first wife in New North Cemetery.

Sarah Pinkham Bunker (1809–1902)

Without mother, father, siblings, or first cousins, Maurice had grown up at 12 Cliff Road (then known as North Street) with only his grandmother, Sarah Pinkham Bunker, for company. "Sarah P." as she was known, worked as a "watcher" by the sickbeds and deathbeds of fellow Nantucketers in order to keep her father's large house—a house inhabited for two decades by only herself and the boy. Then Maurice brought home a bride, and the house began to fill with their children and his wife's relatives. Sarah P. lived on, becoming Nantucket's oldest resident before her death in 1902 at the age of ninety-three.

Sarah P. was reported to have been a good cook. It must have been in the kitchen of 12 Cliff Road during his lonesome childhood that her grandson Maurice learned to make pastry and bake pies.

There is no doubt that grandmother and grandson made mince pies. After all, there is the pie stamp joke, and besides, mince pie is a staple of Nantucket's English culinary heritage. There is a family recipe for venison mincemeat, but Sarah P. and Maurice would have made theirs with beef, there being no deer on Nantucket in all of Sarah P.'s nine decades of life, and only one lone buck in the last months of Maurice's life.

Times have changed, and now people can hardly imagine Nantucket as a deer-free island.

Thousands of years ago, when Nantucket was still part of the mainland, deer roamed right out to the edge of dry land, miles beyond today's South Shore. After rising sea levels separated Nantucket from the mainland, however, isolated animal populations were driven to extinction by indigenous hunters. When the English arrived in 1659, there were no deer on the island, and no moose, bears, wolves, foxes, coyotes, raccoons, skunks, or squirrels either. Nantucket's year-round land-based animals consisted of voles, bats, snakes (and not many kinds of them), and the Wampanoags' dogs. Pesky squirrels have only recently made it to the island, apparently in shipments of lumber. The island remains free of the other critters that are now such a worry to our mainland neighbors, with the notable exception of the white tailed deer.

Nantucket's deer population (and very soon the island's deer problem) had its inception on June 3, 1922, when fishermen rescued an exhausted buck swimming in Nantucket Sound, brought him to the island, and released him. Three and a half years later—on February 23, 1926—summer resident Breckinridge Long purchased two does from Michigan and had them liberated in the vicinity of Squam Swamp to keep the buck company. On April 15, 1935, two more deer were brought to the island "for the purpose of improving the stock." By then the island's inbred herd had become so large and such a menace to farmers' crops that the first deer-hunting season to cull them had been held in February of that very year. The slaughter caused such indignation, however, that an emergency appeal was made to the governor of the Commonwealth of Massachusetts, who closed the season a day after it had opened. Contrary to attempts to reduce the island's herd, three more does were added on April 15, 1936, these being set loose near Trott's Swamp, about as far from Squam Swamp as one can get. Come together they all did, nonetheless, and the herd, the problem, and contrary public opinions persist unabated.

Ours was a hunting family. Men and women alike took up shotguns every fall and winter to hunt for meat whenever opportunity presented itself. We consumed every edible bit of what came home—rabbits, ducks, pheasants, and quail. Aunt Esther was always delighted to receive a deer neck for making this rich and meaty pie filling. In her price list for her Garden Gate Gift Shop, Esther's friend Ellen Ramsdell offered "Mince Meat made from an old Nantucket recipe: Pints $1.25, Quarts $2.25."

Here is the recipe:

ESTHER'S MINCEMEAT

2 lbs. venison or beef, cut up small
1/2 lb. suet, chopped
3 lbs. (about 12) apples put through grinder
1 lb. seedless raisins
1/4 lb. candied citron cut up
1 jar of candied fruits cut up
3 cups granulated sugar
1 cup brown sugar
juice and zest of 1 lemon
juice of 2 oranges and zest of 1 orange
1 teaspoon cloves
2 teaspoons cinnamon
2 teaspoons salt
1 cup vinegar
3 cups apple cider, grape juice, or other fruit juice
brandy and/or rum

Cook meat until tender and put through meat chopper. Add suet and other ingredients except brandy or rum. Cook slowly 4–5 hours, stirring frequently to prevent burning. Add liquor and seal in sterilized jars while hot.

Grampa Gibbs may have made the pastry for his mince pies with a recipe similar to this one from the collection:

ESTHER'S HOT WATER PIE CRUST

1 pound lard at room temperature (very soft)
1 cup hot water
1 tablespoon salt
Pour boiling water on lard
Whip with the salt.
Gradually add 6 cups flour and mix well.

8

*Hilda Sofia Österberg Gibbs (1871–1962) surrounded by
her family in 1918: Maurice Gibbs, Arthur Gibbs,
John Gibbs, Esther Gibbs, and Charlotte Gibbs*

Chapter 2
 Gram

My grandmother was a living presence in my life until I was twenty
years old.

My brothers and I and our five cousins all lived under her roof for some
part of our childhoods, and we called her Gram. My great aunts, who
also stayed with her at 12 Cliff Road off and on over the years, called her
Sister, and often Dear Sister. A Quaker college student from
Pennsylvania who washed dishes in Aunt Esther's restaurant baldly
addressed her as Hilda. His plain speech shocked us, but she didn't
object at all.

Her full name was Hilda Sofia Österberg Gibbs, and she had come to
Nantucket from the west coast of Finland via Chicago, where she had
worked as a housemaid to pay for her transatlantic passage.

She had been born at the end of a deadly famine and at the beginning of
enforcement of a Russification policy in what was then the Russian
Grand Duchy of Finland. Russian troops occupied her town, living in
red-brick barracks. To avoid conscription into the Russian army, local
men were departing *en masse* for North America.

Hilda was the oldest survivor of ten children born to her parents. Their
first child, a girl who came into the world during the famine while the
family still lived in the countryside, did not survive. Four others, born
after the family moved into the town of Vasa, died as well, leaving no
living boys. As the eldest of five daughters, Hilda assumed the
responsibilities of a son, and when her father told her to emigrate to
America and get her sisters there too, she found a family willing to pay
her fare in exchange for work, and off she went.

The year was 1890. With her she took two books: an autograph book in which her school friends wrote messages urging her not to forget them and the Bible she had received at confirmation. As soon as she received her first wages in America, she bought a King James Bible, and by night she taught herself English by comparing passages between the two Bibles.

By the time she married Maurice Gibbs, she had been in this country nine years, and she spoke English fluently, albeit with an accent. Her American-born children described her speech as broken English, and after her death in 1962, they asked me to translate letters she had written in which she had moved back and forth between languages. As the youngest of her grandchildren, left in her company a great deal, I hadn't the slightest problem understanding her — the riveting singer/story-teller of our family.

What seems to be my earliest memory is of standing on a stool next to her at the baking table in her kitchen as she made dinner rolls for Aunt Esther's North Shore Restaurant, a job she undertook for the better part of two decades from when the restaurant first opened in 1943. The daily work of kneading bread kept heart disease and arthritis at bay. When the family doctor finally forbade her to do it anymore, she sat with her hands in her lap, still moving, moving, moving — seeking purpose.

In my memory, we worked side by side, up to our elbows in flour, she wearing an apron printed with big red poppies and I with a towel wrapped around me and secured with a safety pin. Gram would break off a piece of the dinner roll dough and hand it to me to roll into a rectangle. (I inherited her rolling pin and have it to this day.) Then she would give me a brush dipped in melted butter to spread on my piece of dough and a mix of cinnamon and sugar to shake over it. Finally, we would roll it up, and with her big kitchen knife she would slice it into cinnamon rolls to rise again before they went into the baking oven.

Yeast bakery has never intimidated me. We had done it together before I started school.

Gram made only wheat bread, not rye bread, the great Finnish staple. I asked Aunt Esther if she had ever baked rye bread, and Esther had no memory of her mother doing so. The reason is simple enough; rye flour was unavailable on Nantucket. Gram met her craving for rye bread with store-bought Ry-Krisp.

When I looked at the door of Gram's refrigerator, I would salivate. Just thinking about her refrigerator door made me salivate. Even now, I can summon the image, and the Pavlovian response still kicks in. Behind that door there was always a jar of pickled herring, and I can't remember a time when I didn't like it. Afternoons when I came home from elementary school, Gram would make me a little plate of pickled herring on crisp bread. If I brought along a school friend, she would prepare a plate of Ritz crackers with peanut butter and orange marmalade for the other child.

Sometimes we had silvery Jewish-style herring that to me seemed a bit too puckery sharp. When we were lucky, there would be a big jar of reddish *matjessill* with a sweeter and softer taste. One of the local grocery stores still carried it in the 1990s, but no sooner had I returned to live on Nantucket than they discontinued it. Now we have to fetch it from Cambridge whenever we happen to make a trip to Boston.

I have never been served tongue at anyone's home or been offered a tongue sandwich at a picnic, yet beef tongue is available in the meat department of the Nantucket grocery stores. Someone must be cooking it. At our house, tongue was boiled with black peppercorns and a couple of bay leaves. When easily pierced with a fork, it was lifted from the liquid and left in a colander. When cool enough to handle, the rough outer skin peels away easily. We would eat it warm with mashed potatoes. Chilled, it becomes firm, and we would slice it very thin to eat with bread and mustard.

What I used to think of as my grandmother's pickled cucumbers turn out to be every Scandinavian grandmother's pickled cucumbers. The only possible variations are whether one adds any water to the vinegar/sugar mix and whether there is fresh dill on hand or one must make do with chopped parsley.

GRAM'S FRESH PICKLED CUCUMBERS

Score a large cucumber lengthwise all around with the tines of a fork. Slice crossways into paper-thin slices.

Combine 1 cup white vinegar and 2/3 cup sugar. Add salt, pepper, and chopped fresh dill to taste.

Put cucumbers in a glass container and pour vinegar solution over them. Cover and put in cold place overnight before serving.

The cucumbers were often an accompaniment to meatballs and mashed potatoes. As far as my grandmother was concerned, the size of meatballs was of no significance. What was important was to make them from a mixture of ground beef and ground pork. She beat an egg (or several) with milk and added breadcrumbs to absorb the liquid. To flavor the meat she used just salt, white pepper, and onion finely chopped and sautéed before being added to the meat mixture. After shaping the meatballs but before browning them in butter in a skillet, she would roll them in a bit of cornstarch to hold in their juices. Once browned, they went into a heavy pan. She then made cream gravy from the drippings in the skillet, poured it over the meatballs, and let them simmer over low heat as she made mashed potatoes to go with them.

Gram's meatballs were regularly on the North Shore Restaurant menu as Swedish Meatballs, and they were generally popular, but one customer was not at all satisfied. He returned them to the kitchen, saying that they were not authentic because they were too large. He had expected dainty, marble-sized meatballs. Aunt Esther sent word back to the dining room that he was welcome to go up to her mother's kitchen and discuss the matter with her, preferably in Swedish.

A proper accompaniment for meatballs is lingonberry sauce, which we had surprisingly often, considering how difficult and expensive it must have been to get it. More often we had cranberry sauce with them.

Grampa Gibbs and a friend owned and harvested a small cranberry bog off Eel Point Road, so during his lifetime there had always been plenty of cranberries in storage at 12 Cliff Road. They were baked in pies in place of cherries, but the simplest way to use them was in whole-berry sauce.

OLD NANTUCKET WHOLE-CRANBERRY SAUCE

Add one part water to five parts cranberries in a heavy saucepan.

Boil vigorously for five minutes.

Add two or three parts sugar and bring back to a hard boil.

Boil a minute while stirring constantly. If preserving, pour into sterilized jars and seal while hot.

My grandmother and my mother both liked to eat fresh, ripe strawberries with warm buttered rice. I thought this was a waste of good strawberries and never shared their enthusiasm. Later in life I gained a new perspective on this oddity.

Like rye flour, the Scandinavian "pudding rice" (short-grain rice) of my grandmother's childhood was not to be had on Nantucket. Back home, a traditional comfort food was and still is short-grain rice cooked with milk into a smooth porridge and served with an "eye" of butter in the center of each serving. A sprinkle of sugar and cinnamon completes the dish year-round, but in berry season, a sauce of fresh red berries (strawberries, raspberries, or red currants) crushed with sugar is served with the rice porridge.

In Russian cuisine, which has influenced Finnish cuisine, cooked short-grain rice is mixed with sweetened whipped cream flavored with vanilla and a bit of dissolved gelatin. It is then pressed into a ring mold and chilled. To serve, the molded rice is turned out on a plate and the center filled with sweetened berries.

Although I gained insight and appreciation of the rice desserts, I have never been able to acquire a taste for another food beloved of Finns and Swedes then and still now. Called *viili* in Finnish and *fil* in Swedish, a "feely" thing it is. In eastern Finland it is called "long *piimä*." These words are all terms for thickened, soured milk—a relative of buttermilk, yogurt, and sour cream.

A spoonful of the last batch is placed in a shallow dish and unhomogenized milk is poured over it. The dish sits overnight on a shelf in a cool place, and the next day it is ready to eat topped with a bit of sugar and, in season, some berries.

The "long" part has to do with the particular culture for this dish. A spoon dipped in reveals two layers—bright white sour cream on top of something quite different. Lifted on the spoon, it stretches like elastic. It is the string cheese of the yogurt family.

I have never been able to make my way through a serving of it. I eat the sugar and cream layer, add more sugar and berries to the long part and get nowhere. Yet it was dear to my Finnish relatives, and it remains so popular in Finland today that it is produced commercially for sale in the dairy section of supermarkets.

The culture doesn't live forever. It is reputed to be sensitive to weather conditions and liable to die during thunderstorms. When Gram's culture expired, as it did from time to time, she would send to one of her sisters or even to Finland to have a new white cotton handkerchief dipped in a dish of it, dried, and mailed to her. When it arrived, she would pour fresh raw milk over the hanky and start her own new culture.

Much easier to appreciate are pancakes, both cooked on a griddle and baked in the oven. For either kind, Gram's batter was the same: one cup of milk for each egg, sugar, salt, and as little flour as possible. I have never been able to get it to work with simply one cup of flour for each egg and cup of milk. For me it always takes about a half or even three quarters of a cup more of flour. As for the sugar, it is a matter of taste. I use just a quarter cup for a three-egg batter.

The batter needs to stand for at least a few hours and preferably overnight in the refrigerator. Then one can make little silver-dollar pancakes known as *plättar* in Swedish and *lettuja* in Finnish, provided one has a cast-iron pan with round depressions for the pancakes.

Alternatively, the pancake can be baked in the oven. To do this, one melts butter in a cast-iron pan in a 425° oven. Taking the pan out of the oven, one tilts it to be sure the butter covers the entire bottom and then pours the batter into the hot pan. The pan goes right back into the oven for twenty minutes, during which time the pancake puffs and turns golden brown. For large pans, the baking time may be 25 to 30 minutes. This is traditional Thursday fare, eaten along with split pea soup.

Gram had two cookbooks from Finland, both published after she left—one in 1893 and the other in 1900, the latter a classic work by Anna Olsoni. The frontispiece shows three serious-looking women working around a large wood-burning cook stove. Inside the book are schematic drawings of animals showing numbered cuts of meat. The recipes in both books are listed with prices for the individual ingredients and the total price for the each dish. At the beginning of each section is a culinary essay. I never saw Gram consult either book.

Hilda Gibbs and her grandson, Robert Ruley, 1930

Chapter 3
The Great Aunts

Gram's father died in Finland three years after she emigrated. Keeping her parting promise to him, she worked off her own fare and then kept on working to bring her sisters to America. One by one, they all crossed the Atlantic and Americanized their names. They were Elin Mathilda, who became Aunt Ellen; Alma Irene, who became Aunt Irene; Edit Johanna Adolfina, who became Aunt Edith; and Frida Elvira, who became Aunt Frida.

In 1895, Aunt Ellen had joined Gram and was working on Nantucket along with a friend and age-mate from Finland, a woman named Ida Gref, to whom was extended the courtesy title of Aunt Ida. Within five years, Aunt Irene and Aunt Edith had joined them. Aunt Frida was the last to come. By 1910, the sisters and their friend Ida had all moved on to lives on the mainland.

Aunt Ellen died in 1916, and over the years so many of her sisters' grandchildren and great-grandchildren have been named for her that ours is a family full of Ellens. It can be confusing.

Aunt Irene settled in East Providence, married, and raised a family of five cousins with whom we stayed in touch.

Gram had a maternal aunt named Magdalena Berg, who served as an army nurse in the 1870s during the early days of professionalized nursing. When Gram left for America, Aunt Magdalena gave her a wooden box from Turkey to take with her as a memento. Perhaps inspired by their aunt's example, Gram helped Aunt Edith enroll in nursing school, after which Edith remained unmarried and had a nursing career in Philadelphia.

Not long ago I was told that Aunt Frida also enrolled in nursing school, but gave it up for marriage and raising a family.

Hilda Gibbs surrounded by her sisters: Edith, Irene, Ellen, and Frida Österberg. Her children are Arthur (b. 1900) and Richard (d. 1904 at age 15 months).

All the sisters came and brought their families for summer visits at 12 Cliff Road. They would sit, chat, and knit by the hour, sometimes joined by Gram's oldest son. Uncle Arthur was the only man I ever knew who knitted, although I have been told that shipboard knitting is about as common as basket making and scrimshandering.

I have no personal memory of Aunt Irene, but among the recipes I have inherited there is Potato Flour Cake attributed to some aunt; the "Aunt" is clear, the name illegible. Potato flour, a staple of Scandinavian cooking, hasn't been readily available on Nantucket, and Gram substituted cornstarch for potato flour in most of her cooking. For this recipe real potato flour is needed.

POTATO FLOUR CAKE

Combine 2 eggs, well beaten, with 1 cup sugar and beat together for ten minutes.
Sift together:
1/2 cup potato flour
1/2 cup bread flour
1 teaspoon baking powder
A pinch of salt
Mix the dry ingredients into the egg mixture and flavor with vanilla.
Add 1/2 cup of hot milk last.
Bake for twenty minutes.

No pan size or oven temperature is specified in the recipe as written. It works well baked at 350° in a greased and floured 8-inch square pan. The result is a soft, sweet, white cake resembling angel food cake and is good served with fresh berries macerated with a bit of sugar and a drop of balsamic vinegar.

When I was around twelve years old, my mother became disabled and could no longer cook. That summer, Aunt Edith taught me to take over in the kitchen. Her instruction was not a matter of measures, temperatures, and times. I recall the frustration of being told to add flour to the pancake batter "until it feels right." I would show her the bowl of batter and ask if it was right only to be told that it was not a matter of how it looked but of how it felt. I survived and could soon make all kinds of pancakes to say nothing of Yorkshire pudding and popovers. Before she departed in September, I could also roast meat and fry fish.

As a reward, Aunt Edith promised to knit me a blue sweater. I looked forward to it with great anticipation, but the execution fell short of expectation. The sweater was a failure, not the first or last of Aunt

Edith's unsatisfactory sweaters. An olive green and magenta one she made for my father was infamous.

Aunt Edith had a rare type of color blindness. She could discern color intensity but not hue, which led to odd mismatches in her knitting when one skein of yarn came to an end and she took up another. In spite of this, or perhaps because of it, six years after the disappointment of the never-worn blue sweater, she crocheted for me an afghan to take to college. The squares are made from light blue, dark blue, black, brown, and yellow yarn—undoubtedly what she happened to have in her basket. The charm is that, search as one will, there is absolutely no pattern to be discerned. Repairs made over the years are undetectable. I have always cherished the afghan, which more than made up for the botched sweater.

Along with everyday and Sunday dishes, Aunt Edith gave me complicated instructions for making fruit soup.

Fruit soup is a dish shared by Scandinavians and Russians. In the West it is called *soppa*, and in the East it is called *kisel'*. Finland inclines eastward on this one and borrows the Russian word as *kiisseli*. Whatever one calls it, fruit soup is simply fruit juice or stewed fruit in its cooking water, in either case thickened with potato flour. Typically, making fruit soup involves buying a package of mixed dried fruit or dried apricots, popping the fruit into a pot of water, adding some cinnamon and maybe sugar or honey, and cooking the fruit until soft. Then the fruit is lifted out of the pot and set aside, while to the remaining liquid is added some potato flour (or cornstarch) that has been stirred into some cold water. After a bit of simmering, the fruit syrup thickens and becomes clear. Then it is poured over the fruit in a dessert bowl and may be served with sweetened whipped cream.

This was not Aunt Edith's approach to fruit soup. Hers was more like what Russians would call a compote. It began with apple syrup and had other cooked fruits added to it.

AUNT EDITH'S FRUIT SOUP

Peel, core, and boil fresh apples with sugar until the apples disintegrate.
Strain the liquid and discard the apple pulp.
Add more sugar and cook until the syrup thickens.
Flavor with lemon juice.

Cook other fresh or dried fruit separately, each according to its own cooking time.
Fruits to be used alone or in combination, as available:
Pears
Peaches
Apricots
Cherries
Raisins
Currants
Strawberries

Add the cooked fruits to the apple syrup, return to low heat, and thicken with tapioca.

To make a smooth soup, put the cooked fruits through a sieve or food mill before adding to the apple syrup.

I have made Aunt Edith's fruit soup from time to time and can't imagine why anyone would cook strawberries at all. I also think that lemon zest is an improvement over lemon juice in the apple syrup. Surely the tapioca as a thickening agent is a substitute for potato flour. Cornstarch would do as well.

Great Aunt Edith Österberg at home in Philadelphia

Like Aunt Irene, Aunt Frida and her family lived in Rhode Island. Not only was Frida fifteen years younger than Gram, she was younger than her husband and not far advanced in years when he died. In her widowhood, she pursued an independent life before returning to Rhode Island to reside in an assisted living facility. I went to visit her there, taking along a loaf of freshly baked cardamom bread. In Finland this ubiquitous coffee bread is known as *pulla*, no matter whether it is baked as individual round buns (Swedish *bullar*) or as a long braid.

As I walked through the door to her studio apartment, Aunt Frida was just taking a *pulla* braid out of the oven in her little galley kitchen. When I showed her what I had brought, she asked, "Who taught you how to make that?" and we had a good laugh. Her cardamom braid seemed tastier than mine.

The trick is to grind cardamom to just the right degree of coarseness with a proper spice grinder. If it is too fine, it just disappears, while smashing very hard whole cardamom seeds by hand in a mortar yields tooth-endangering grit. Plastic tubes of cardamom ground exactly right for baking are readily available in Sweden and Finland. If cardamom isn't available, the bread can be flavored with vanilla.

CARDAMOM BRAIDS

Beat 1 egg with 3/4 cup of sugar, a pinch of salt, and ground cardamom or vanilla.

Add 1 tablespoon of dry yeast and set aside for 5 minutes.

Heat 2 cups milk until pleasantly warm to the touch, not hot.

Measure 7 cups of good flour into another bowl.

Add the milk to the eggs/yeast/sugar mixture, beat with a whisk, and then add enough of the flour to make a mixture with the consistency of oatmeal.

Melt one stick of butter or margarine. It doesn't have to be completely melted. If it gets sizzling hot, it will kill the yeast.

Add the melted butter/margarine to the dough.

Add most of the rest of the flour, working it in with hands or a wooden spoon.

Pile the remaining flour on a good surface, turn the dough out on it, and knead, the longer the better.

Wash out the dough bowl in hot water. Dry it, and butter it.

Put the dough back in the bowl and then flip it over, so it is buttered on both sides.

Cover with a towel and let rise until double.

Punch the dough down and divide it in half. Divide each half into three parts and make into long ropes. Raisins can be added to the bread at this point, rolled into the inside of the dough ropes.

On two lightly greased baking sheets, make two braids.

Cover and let rise until double. Sliced almonds can be stuck into the braids at this time.

Bake the braids one at a time in a 400 ° oven for about 20 minutes until golden and crusty.

Brush with beaten egg and water to add a shine, and sprinkle with pearl sugar.

Cool on wire racks.

The women in Gram's family survived a childhood fraught with dangers and then as adults managed on their own for years at a time. With the exception of Aunt Ellen, they lived well into old age. Back in Finland, my great-grandmother, Ulrika Österberg, outlived her husband by thirty-three years. Gram used to say that women should look for husbands younger than themselves, since men are not so durable.

As a child among many robust old women, I observed them with the thought that youth and middle age probably take care of themselves; the challenging part comes toward the end.

Cousins on the deck of the Anglers Club, 2000
Frances Karttunen, Ellen Kindstedt, Maurice Gibbs,
Millicent Gibbs, Ellen Gibbs Holdgate

Chapter 4
Girl Cousins

Like myself, all my first cousins at one time or another lived for a while with Gram in the house at 12 Cliff Road. Because of the age spread among us, we girl cousins lived with Gram one at a time. As adults, we have learned from each other by sharing memories. As the youngest, my earliest recollections sometimes seem dubious. There has always been an air of excitement and revelation in comparing them with Cousin Ellen's or Cousin Betty's and learning that they match.

Cousin Betty was born in 1922, a year before my parents' marriage. She went to live at Gram's house when she was eight years old and stayed for three years.

During those years Gram made soft molasses cookies that Betty recalls as the best she ever had. Her father's new wife wanted to learn how to make them, but Gram's directions for cooking never included measurements or times; everything was done by eye and feel. After Betty left 12 Cliff Road, she and her stepmother tried to replicate the molasses cookies, but every attempt ended in failure. By the time I was a child in her house, Gram had stopped baking cookies altogether, and I have no idea what these special ones were like.

When Cousin Betty was a little girl, she adored my father because he would stand at the kitchen sink opening quahogs and giving her as many as she pleased. From before we cousins could remember, we considered raw oysters, clams, and scallops a treat and joked about eating them so fresh they wiggled on the way down.

When my late father-in-law visited Nantucket in the 1970s and we dined together at the Jared Coffin House, I ordered him a half-dozen littlenecks on the half shell. As he slid one off its shell into his mouth, a look of panic crossed his face. He managed to swallow it and graciously gave the other five to me.

In the 1980s a colleague from IBM France took a bunch of us out for an expense-account dinner at a Paris seafood restaurant. First he ordered me a plate of periwinkles that came with a hatpin to extract them from their shells. When I finished them off, he ordered limpets, and I ate them too. His final challenge was a single bright-orange creature that was tasty and probably very expensive. When I downed it, the whole table cheered. Cousin Betty would have been proud.

Betty was Gram's first grandchild, and I — born twenty years later — was her last. In between were my two brothers, three boy cousins, and one girl: Cousin Ellen Gibbs.

Hilda Gibbs with granddaughter Ellen Gibbs
in the backyard of 12 Cliff Road, 1940

Ellen was seven years older than I, just the right age to look after me the summer before I went to first grade. Ellen had her first camera, and I became her model. I had never before been into the fields between Cliff Road and North Liberty Street. That June the fields were thick with daisies that seemed to come up to my chin. Ellen took my hand and led me among them, pinned a wreath of daisies in my hair, and photographed me, documenting my first venture away from home without a grown-up. By September I was on my own. On the first day of first grade, Mother walked me to Academy Hill School and left me there to make my way home with the other neighborhood children.

Frances Ruley photographed by her cousin Ellen Gibbs in 1948

Born in 1935, Cousin Ellen was an independent child, a little on the wild side, capable of sneaking out at night and filching cigarettes. Because of her irrepressible giggle, Cousin Betty thought of Cousin Ellen as a dizzy blonde.

Despite her giggle, Ellen had a deep side. She had firsthand memories of the late years of the Depression and acute ones of life on Nantucket during World War II. As a wife and mother in the Vietnam era, she wrote a memoir, "Will the Planes Come Tonight?" about the fearsome wartime years of her late childhood, telling about blackouts, air raid drills, refugees, rationing, and her fear of low-flying aircraft. In conclusion, she recalled the end of World War II: "It meant real ice cream again with sprills. No more air raids, no more worry in the eyes of the grown-ups. Now all the shadows were gone. But were they really? Damn the war."

Soon after Ellen wrote this, she returned to Nantucket where she lived the rest of her life, rarely traveling off-island. She cooked prodigiously for family gatherings. Here is a recipe I have reconstructed of a dish she served as an appetizer. Most Nantucket scallop appetizers involve bacon or cheese. This one is notable for including neither.

COUSIN ELLEN'S SCALLOPS

Preheat the broiler.
Butter six broiler-proof individual-serving baking dishes.
Very lightly sauté 1 pound of bay scallops in butter.
Season the scallops with celery salt and put into the baking dishes.
In the same pan, sauté one large or two small shallots.
Toss the shallots and butter with breadcrumbs. (Panko style works well.)
Spread the warm breadcrumb mixture on top of the scallops.
Run them under the broiler until the breadcrumb topping is nicely browned.
Serve with lemon wedges.

Ellen's special gifts lay elsewhere than cooking, however. She had a remarkable ability to look at a thing, see exactly how it was made, and replicate it without a pattern. She took great pleasure in painting and was, beyond all else, passionate about freshwater fishing.

Close to the end of her life she wrote to me:

> *It's always been very special to have lived at 12 North Street*
> *(Cliff Road). I had many firsts there: I lost my first tooth there*
> *and found out there was no Santa when I was six. I got my*
> *first set of oil paints from Aunt Esther at age twelve, and I got*
> *my first grown-up lady's slip from Esther too. I heard the*
> *word "sex" for the first time from a boy cutting grass in*
> *Gram's strawberry patch and didn't know what it meant. I*
> *had my first date to go to a prom. I had my first roast pig at*
> *Thanksgiving, the whole pig with an apple in its mouth.*

In our family of multiple Ellens, there is also Cousin Ellen Kindstedt of the Rhode Island branch of our family. She and I share a common great-grandmother, Ulrika Österberg, who lived and died in Finland. Cousin Ellen Kindsedt and I were born within a few months of each other, and we look alike, sharing with many of our other cousins what we have come to think of as the Österberg look. (Both my Cousin Maurice and I have had the experience of going to meet relatives in Finland wondering whether we would be able to pick them out in the crowd meeting the boat and then, to our surprise and relief, recognizing them instantly.)

When Cousin Ellen Kindstedt and I compared notes about the food in Gram's and Aunt Frida's households, they matched nearly item for item: the coffee bread, the meatballs, the pickled herring. The one difference was that her family ate *limpa* bread.

In Helsinki, during the autumn herring festival, boats come to the city harbor from islands all around to sell fish and limpa. It is a sweet, dark bread made with rye flour, molasses, anise seed, and orange peel. We never had it at 12 Cliff Road for the good reason that rye flour was not available on Nantucket. I doubt that Aunt Frida baked it herself either, because it is difficult to make at home. I am sure she bought it from a neighborhood Swedish bakery. Cranston, where the Kindstedt family lived, is home to the Rhode Island Swedish Heritage Association, and where there are Swedes, there are Swedish bakers. (When I first arrived in Texas, I was delighted to discover a Swedish bakery right in Austin where I could buy limpa.)

While I spent the summer of 1963 in Finland, Cousin Ellen Kindstedt waited on table at the North Shore Restaurant, yet another bonding experience for the two of us when we compare notes about our young lives.

Cousin Karen Gibbs is my second cousin. We didn't share the experience of living at 12 Cliff Road, but we do share the family lore that carries on. When we meet on the street or at the post office, we have a world to talk about.

Once we were holding forth about air-drying laundry. I had heard that one of Nantucket's housing developments has a covenant prohibiting drying one's wash outdoors. We were both scandalized. With all the sun and wind we have for free, it seems outrageous to run energy-consuming dryers on fair, dry days.

To Cousin Karen I muttered about a yellow paint stain I could not get out of a pair of white pants, and she waxed lyrical about the effectiveness of fog washing. The next time it's really foggy, she advised, hang those pants out on the line and let them get thoroughly soaked. Leave them there until the sun comes out again and dries them, and the yellow will probably be gone. That is how Nantucketers used to bleach their household linens, spreading them over bushes in the fog.

When the late journalist Mary Miles interviewed people, she would almost always ask, "What is your favorite place on Nantucket?" I always wanted her to put that question to me, and she never did. As a child, I helped Gram hang out the wash, and these days my favorite spot on the island is my own clothes yard, right out my back door. On good days it is filled with sunshine and breeze. There are peonies in the middle, flowers along both sides, and a grape arbor across the back. In the summer the grapevines cover the arbor with a green leafy roof, and neighbors who live upstairs in the building behind ours tell me that they enjoy looking down on my clothes yard from above.

The arbor supports three varieties of grapes—Concord, red, and white— that Ellen Ramsdell and Aunt Esther planted half a century ago. In September they yield so much fruit I have to call in jelly makers from all over the island to take away boxes and shopping bags full for their own purposes. Still, there is enough for a year's supply of jelly for us. I've made up names for different combinations of the three varieties: Blush, Rosé, Red-White-and-Concord, Lily Pond Blend.

A corner of the arbor and the clothes yard is visible from North Centre Street. During the time when my husband and I were still at the University of Texas, we could only come home after the end of spring term in May. People would call or drop by as soon as they caught sight of wash drying out on the line. Once they knew we had arrived, they would issue reminders to get our window boxes up and planted by Memorial Day, and once I was given an impromptu lecture about hanging my laundry correctly (towels at the end visible from the street, underwear out of sight, bathing suits anywhere we pleased).

Eugene Joseph Ruley (1901–1967) opening littlenecks

Chapter 5
The Boss

My father, Eugene Joseph Ruley, came to Nantucket as a Navy radioman and stayed for the rest of his life. He was nicknamed The Boss and was often addressed and recalled as Boss Ruley. As a building contractor managing a crew, he surely was the boss, but within our matriarchal household, Gram was boss until the mantle passed to Aunt Esther.

Unlike Gram, my father did not tell stories of life before Nantucket. He came from Baltimore, and he kept in touch with sisters and a brother there. He and my mother once went to visit them, and what my mother recalled most vividly of Baltimore were the early-morning calls of the street vendors. Aunts Mary and Julia were active in Baltimore politics and took my parents along to a boisterous smoke-filled ward meeting that my mother found intimidating. Later on, my brother Bob got to know them, and when his second daughter was born, he named her Julia. My single contact with these aunts was a manicure set I once received from one of them as a Christmas gift. The scissors were uncommonly sharp and useful, and they resided in my sewing box for decades.

From documents preserved and passed on to me, I know that my father was the eighth child born to Stephen P. and Annie M. Ruley. His birth on November 11, 1901, was at home, attended by a midwife named Mary Stein. On the Baltimore Return of a Birth form, his father's name is spelled Stephan and his mother's maiden name is Buenker, while on his death certificate, his father's name is spelled Stephen and his mother's maiden name is given as Binger. A 1938 letter concerning a piece of property in Baltimore confirms that he had a paternal great aunt named Elizabeth Eberle.

I have the impression from imperfect childhood memories that my
father's mother did not long survive his birth, and because his sisters
and brothers were unable to care for an infant, my father was placed in a
Catholic orphanage for children of German Catholic heritage. That
would have been St. Anthony's Orphan Asylum (founded in 1854 and in
operation until 1943), where the Sisters of Notre Dame looked after
eighty to a hundred small children at a time.

It is possible that when he was old enough to be taught a trade, he
moved on to St. Mary's Industrial School for Boys, which was founded in
1866 and remained in operation until 1950. The most famous of its
"inmates," as the boys were called, was Babe Ruth, who was committed
to St. Mary's in 1902 at the age of seven. Each boy at St. Mary's was
taught a trade, among the choices being carpentry. Whether at St. Mary's
or elsewhere, my father received training in carpentry and
cabinetmaking while still in his teens. He also acquired a lifelong passion
for baseball.

Born in 1901, he was a sliver too young for the trench warfare of World
War I, but he joined the Navy as soon as he could and was sent to the
U.S. Naval Radio School in Great Lakes, Illinois. Graduating from there
in the summer of 1920, he came to Nantucket, where the Surfside Life-
Saving Station had been converted into a naval radio-compass facility.
Three years later he married my mother, an eleventh-generation
Nantucketer on Grampa Gibbs's side of the family, and here he stayed.

Overage for combat in World War II, he enrolled in the Coast Guard
Reserve in 1943. As a Radio Technician first class with the rank of
coxswain in Flotilla 604, Nantucket, he served until September 1945. I
have no recollection of his military service, and like his childhood in
Baltimore, it was not something he ever spoke of.

If my father relayed next to nothing to us about Baltimore in words, he did so in what were to us exotic foodways.

Stewed tomatoes were not part of Gram's household cuisine, but my father adored them. What is more, he sprinkled his tomatoes with sugar before tucking in.

It was my father who was responsible for the roast suckling pig one Thanksgiving. Never had the Nantucket family experienced such a thing as a whole piglet on a platter with cranberry eyes and an apple in its mouth. Juice and fat extruded from the eye sockets ran like tears down the piglet's cheeks and seemed so pathetic that the Nantucketers found it difficult to think of it as dinner. Gram had roasted a turkey as an alternative, and Cousin Ellen recalled that "by the way, I took turkey."

Eugene Ruley with Charlotte Ruley, Esther Gibbs, and Robert Ruley at the beach in 1927

One autumn my father and a buddy of his bought a full-grown hog and set about curing their own bacon and hams. I don't recall how the hams turned out, but the bacon was inedible.

The same friend and my father bought twenty Guinea hens with the intention of letting the flock grow on its own to provide the occasional Sunday dinner. The birds were very tasty, however, and proved all too easy to grab, so in no time we had eaten our way through all twenty without waiting for eggs and chicks.

Nantucket cuisine had always tended to the plain and parsimonious, even more so during and immediately following the Great Depression. Its goodness depended on freshness and simplicity. Perhaps my father's most enduring contribution was a passion for the best of everything and in abundance. For holidays we always had mixed nuts and fruit, both fresh and dried. There was steamed fig pudding with hard sauce and foamy egg sauce, both flavored with whiskey, and to drink there was sweet, thick, homemade eggnog topped with fresh-shaved nutmeg. Given such heart-stopping fare, only the hard physical work we all did between holidays kept us alive.

The most enduring culinary legacy from my father is the tradition of Christmas oysters. Whatever else was served at Christmas, there had to be oysters. My father's preference was for rich oyster stew. At Christmastime in New England there were no fresh green onions or parsley to chop as a garnish for the stew, but paprika added color to the presentation.

MARYLAND OYSTER STEW

Shuck oysters and reserve their liquor.

Strain the oyster liquor through a fine sieve twice to remove any sand or bits of shell.

Gently warm the strained liquor together with light cream (about a quart of cream to each pint of oysters). Do not permit this liquid to boil.

Gently sauté the oysters in melted butter, just until the oysters curl.

Pour the warm liquid over the oysters, stirring gently.

Season with salt and ground black pepper.

Ladle into warm shallow soup plates and add a dash of ground paprika.

During the three decades I lived in Central Texas, oysters from the Gulf of Mexico were always available and inexpensive. Instead of oyster stew, our own Christmas Day oyster tradition has been fried oysters with lemon wedges.

For three years my parents and I lived in an upstairs apartment on Whale Street, in a building that stood in the middle of what is now the grocery store parking lot on Straight Wharf. (To make way for the parking lot, the street was relocated and named New Whale Street.) My father would have been delighted to know that there had once been an oyster house on our street, as advertised in the *Nantucket Inquirer* in 1833.

NEW EATING-HOUSE.

The subscriber informs his friends and the public, and especially his former customers, that he has opened for their accommodation a new Cook-shop and Refectory, at No. 5 Whale street; where he is now ready to furnish Oysters, Pastry, and other refreshments in every variety of cookery, at the shortest notice, and in a style not inferior to that of any other establishment of the kind in town.

He would further state that having pledged himself to the owner of the building, George Myrick Esq., to keep no ardent spirits of any description for sale—and thus having relinquished an important portion of the usual profits of such an establishment, he hopes for an increased patronage in that line of his business to which he intends to confine his attention.

Pies, Tarts, Custards, Oysters roasted and fried, stewed, or in soup, Fish chowder, Hot Chocolate and Coffee, Mush and Milk, Beer, Cider, &c. at all seasonable hours—and any extra entertainment for parties, &c. will be supplied according to order, on reasonable terms and with every attention to the wishes of his guests.

Feb. 23.   3w   JACOB JONES.

Chapter 6
Mother

My mother, Charlotte, had a transcontinental namesake. This we only
learned when an old photo in a pewter frame passed to one of my nieces.
I had always imagined the woman in the studio portrait to be great-
great-grandmother Sarah P. Bunker herself, but my niece teased the
photo out of the frame and on the back we read, "Cousin Lottie.
Charlotte was named for her."

Charlotte Amelia Pinkham Hamblen (1846–1902)

Charlotte Amelia Pinkham, born in 1846, was the daughter of Sarah P.'s
brother Peter Pinkham and his wife, Judith. When Lottie was nine years
old, her mother died and her father left the island. After the Civil War,
Lottie and Charles E. Hamblen of New York were wed in Boston, and
they eventually moved to Spokane, Washington. The year of their
marriage, 1869, was the year Grampa Gibbs was born.

Despite the continent between them, Cousin Lottie and her Nantucket
family remained in touch. When Sarah P. died in 1902, some of the

family furniture was shipped from 12 Cliff Road to Spokane. Alas, Cousin Lottie did not live to enjoy it. Before the end of the year she, too, had died. When my mother was born three years later, my grandparents named her Charlotte Hamblen Gibbs.

Charlotte grew up an island-loving girl. In October 1922 the *Inquirer and Mirror* published "Our Swiftest Season," an essay she had written at the beginning of her senior year in Nantucket High School. She wrote:

> *If only the summer visitors knew the witching charm of Nantucket when the colors are all flying and the air is just frosty enough to bite cheeks and nip fingers, then they would spend not only the summer but part of the winter here. Some of the best of them, however, have found it out, and we are glad to have them linger. They seem to belong in a way. Our name for them is "On-from-Off."*

She had her complaints about summer visitors however.

> *Houses to be rented receive an extra spring polish. If you are unlucky enough to be living in one, you know how renters always come to look it over at the wrong time; and how they insist on seeing the room where you are dressing, or the kitchen at dinner time.*

In the summer, Nantucket families relinquished their homes to the visitors and had

> *to move into cramped quarters until September. Then we are free again, and our village, our commons, and the whole of our island is ours until another visiting season begins.*

In the body of her essay, Charlotte, identifying herself as "a surfman's daughter," enumerated the island's Life-Saving Stations with their equipment. She described the crews' gun drills, communication drills, and boat drills, the last of which consisted of "launching, manning, and landing of the surf-boat in the surf." Two months after the publication of her essay Grampa Gibbs was dead of injuries sustained in a boat drill.

If going off-island for further education had ever been an option, it was dashed by her father's death. Charlotte graduated from high school the following June and married Radioman Eugene Ruley in August. My brother Bob was born the next summer.

My mother had been a wizard at self-education from childhood. She was an enthusiastic birder with binoculars and books, but she also knew a great deal about birds from shooting them and preparing them for the table. In cold weather there were often black ducks, teal, and pheasants hung on the side of the house. When they were to be cooked, we took them down and plucked them, taking time to examine their plumage, beaks, eyes, and feet. With the feathers off, Mother would open the main cavity and pull out the guts, being careful not to break the gall bladder. From the neck cavity she would extract the crop, and we would open it together, seeing what the bird's last meal had been. Sometimes there were tiny snail shells in the crop mixed with the grit birds consume to grind their food.

My parents preferred to cook game birds quickly in a hot oven so the meat was pink and juicy upon carving. In his later years my brother Bob acquired a press to extract the juice from duck breasts.

Charlotte Hamblen Gibbs Ruley (1905–1970)

Mother was also a self-taught botanist, knowing the full range of island plants by their common and Latin names. It was with tremendous enthusiasm that she introduced me to a shy white and green flower growing in pine needles: a specimen of *Chimaphila maculata*. Its common name was just as much fun to say: Pipsissewa.

She was a forager for edible wild plants. We would pick blueberries and beach plums by the bucketful, and while we were doing it, we chewed on checkerberry leaves. Of checkerberry, Alice Albertson wrote in 1921, "A low evergreen that one greets with enthusiasm, for the oval leaves have a deliciously spicy flavor (one often encountered in toothpaste, for instance)." We ate the pencil-thin stalks of naturalized asparagus growing in the cemeteries, and when we weeded nut grass out of flowerbeds, we brushed dirt off the little tubers on the roots and ate them too. Their taste is on the bitter side, but we believed that

Nantucket's Wampanoags ate them, and that gave them cachet. (As it turns out *Cyperus rotundus* is an alien invader originating in Africa.)

My mother was equally enthusiastic about wild mushrooms, although she limited herself to gathering just one kind, the meadow mushroom, *Agaricus campestris*, for which she would hunt on golf courses. Once, she found one larger than our skillet, and no one else in the family would touch a bite of it. They watched her all day for signs of poisoning, but she was just fine.

In Finland, my late father-in-law — as ardent about mushrooms as Mother had been — took me out with him and taught me to recognize many different kinds of safe edible mushrooms. I once found a large Hen of the Woods and carried it to him, asking "Is this a good one?" His eyes crinkled up with pleasure as he exclaimed "Oh yes!" One of the ways Mother used mushrooms was in a bluefish dish of her own devising.

CHARLOTTE'S BLUEFISH CASSEROLE

Heat the oven to 375°.
Butter a casserole dish.
Make a white sauce seasoned with salt and pepper.
Grate plenty of Gruyère cheese.
Sauté sliced mushrooms in a little butter.
Pour some white sauce into the bottom of the casserole.
Place skinless bluefish fillets in the casserole.
Add a layer of mushrooms.
Pour more white sauce over the mushrooms.
Add a layer of grated cheese.
Sprinkle the top with breadcrumbs.
Bake about 30 minutes until the breadcrumbs are browned, the cheese is melted, and the fish is cooked.

The traditional Fourth of July meal was salmon with egg sauce and fresh green peas. I have a vivid memory of shelling peas on a summer evening, sitting on a step next to a large woman in a summer dress who was also shelling peas. As I split each pod with a fingernail and then pushed the peas out with my thumb, the peas plunked into a metal basin at our feet and the empty pod dropped silently into a brown paper bag.

 During my childhood, dinner was at noon on weekdays and at one P.M. on Sundays and holidays. If the peas we were shelling that evening were for Independence Day dinner, they would have gone into cool storage overnight.

In the late morning Mother would prepare the fish and egg sauce. Like white sauce, her egg sauce was made of flour blended with melted butter, but the liquid for the sauce was fish stock rather than milk, giving it a shiny look. To it she added chopped hard-boiled eggs, and she seasoned it with salt and coarsely ground black pepper. The bright green peas and the pink fish with its sauce were a pretty sight.

The first time I passed a Fourth of July in Finland, I served salmon and peas to my friends, who were polite about the egg sauce but not enthusiastic.

For festive occasions in Finland, salmon and eggs are encased in pastry, and the dish goes by the Russian name of *kulibiaka*. The chilled pastry is rolled out in a rectangle on a pastry cloth or waxed paper. A bed of cooked rice is laid down the center, sliced hard-boiled eggs are layered on top of the rice, and lightly poached salmon goes on top of the eggs. The salmon is sprinkled with a bit of coarsely ground sea salt and plenty of chopped fresh dill. Finally, another layer of rice is laid on top, and the pastry is gently folded up and sealed around the filling. The sides are folded and tucked in, and the pastry cloth/waxed paper is used to gently turn the kulibiaka onto a baking sheet, seam side down. Decorations can be made from scraps of left-over pastry and attached to the top with egg wash (an egg beaten with a bit of water). Then the whole kulibiaka is brushed with egg wash and pricked with a fork (to let steam escape without breaking the crust) before being baked in a 375° oven for about thirty-five minutes until golden. As soon as it comes piping hot from the oven, it is served with pickled cucumbers and lemon wedges.

I use a cream cheese pastry for kulibiaka.

CREAM CHEESE PASTRY

1/2 cup unsalted butter
2 tablespoons whole milk
1/2 teaspoon salt
4 ounces cream cheese
1 1/4 cups flour

Leave the butter and cream cheese to soften at room temperature for an hour. Cream them together with a wooden spoon until they are completely blended. Blend in the milk with a wooden spoon. Sift flour and salt together onto the butter/cheese/milk paste and work in with wooden spoon. Gently work to form a ball of sticky, soft dough. Lightly flour the ball, wrap it in waxed paper, and chill overnight. Roll out the next day.

This same pastry can also be used for making turnovers filled with mushroom/sour cream filling, venison mincemeat, or mashed sweet potato flavored with nutmeg. For Christmas stars, the rolled-out pastry is cut into rectangles with slit corners. A spoonful of prune filling goes in the middle of each rectangle. Then every other point is turned up to make a pinwheel. Turnovers and Christmas stars are brushed with egg wash and baked in a 400° oven for 12–15 minutes.

All these pastries are best served warm from the oven, but my mother's
Christmas fruitcake was another matter altogether. Preparation began
before Thanksgiving, with the cake soaking up rum until Christmas.

TRADITIONAL FRUITCAKE
This is a recipe for a 5 1/2 pound cake.

Soak the following fruits overnight in 1/2 cup dark Puerto Rican rum:
1 pound candied pineapple
1/2 pound candied cherries
1/4 pound candied citron
1/8 pound candied lemon peel
1/8 pound. candied orange peel
1 pound golden raisins
1/2 pound seedless dark raisins
1/4 pound currants

*The next step is to line the bottom of a tube pan with heavy brown paper cut
from a shopping bag (not one with printing on it). Place the pan on the brown
paper and trace around the outside edge with a pencil. Then stick the pencil
down the hole and trace around the inside edge. Cut out and trim so it slides
down the cone and sits on the bottom of the pan.*

*Now do something Mother never did: spray the paper with baking spray so the
cake won't stick to it. Also spray the whole inside of the tube pan.*

Coarsely chop the following nuts:
1/4 pound blanched shelled almonds (not salted)
1/4 pound shelled walnuts or pecans

Set oven at 275°.

Sift 2 cups flour and very gently measure out 1 1/2 cups by dipping it into a measuring cup with a spoon. Sift it again onto a sheet of waxed paper with the following ingredients:

1/2 teaspoon mace
1/2 teaspoon cinnamon
1/2 teaspoon baking soda

Mix the remaining 1/2 cup of flour with fruits in a large bowl. (Coating them with flour keeps them from sticking together.)

Beat 5 eggs slightly.

Measure 1 tablespoon of milk and 1 teaspoon almond extract together into a cup.

Cream together with hands (not with a wooden spoon):

1/4 pound butter
1 cup sugar

When these are light and well mixed, add 1 cup brown sugar (firmly packed) and keep working with hands until light and fluffy.

Now using a wooden spoon, mix in the beaten eggs, the milk/almond mixture, and the flour thoroughly. Pour this mixture over the fruits and nuts and mix together with hands. Fill the pan with the mixture, pressing down to be sure there are no air pockets.

Bake 3 hours and 15 minutes.

Let stand 30 minutes after taking it from the oven. Then turn upside down on a wire rack, remove the pan, and carefully peel off the paper.

48

Wrap the cake in cheesecloth and store in a covered container in a cool place for several weeks or a month, dousing it with rum every week or so.

Thanks to my mother's intense intellectual curiosity that she happily shared with me, the first ten years of my life, lived at 12 Cliff Road and in my parents' little cottage behind it on Kite Hill, were full of investigations, experiments, and discoveries. School was almost incidental.

Esther Ulrika Gibbs (1911–1993) and Peggy

Chapter 7
Aunt Esther

Aunt Esther Ulrika Gibbs was the baby of the family. Born in the summer of 1911, she wears a skeptical look even in her baby pictures. As a child she detested dresses and hair ribbons. Her fervent wish was to have been exchanged at birth with her friend and schoolmate Emily Coffin, so Emily could have the bows and the frills, while Esther could wear overalls and tend the Coffin family's sheep in 'Sconset.

She was not fond of her name either. Esther was the name of a good friend of Gram's back in Finland, and Ulrika was Gram's mother's name. It was her middle name that bothered Aunt Esther most. She signed her name "Esther U. Gibbs," and if asked what the U. stood for, she would say her middle name was Useless. It was only late in life, when she read a biography of the Swedish Queen Ulrika Eleanora, that she felt reconciled to her full name.

Even before Grampa Gibbs died, Gram was taking in summer visitors and serving them afternoon tea. Soon after she was widowed, Gram had additions made to the house at 12 Cliff Road to accommodate even more guests and began paying an annual fee for a common victualler's license. That was how Aunt Esther began her own career, helping to prepare and serve the late-afternoon fare in her own home.

In her mid-teens she went to work at the Roberts House on Centre Street, first in the kitchen and then as one of the uniformed waitresses in the dining room. Leaving school before graduation, she left home to work in Florida resorts for several winters, determined to learn the restaurant business and to build capital to open a restaurant of her own on Nantucket.

The Depression intervened, and then came World War II. Aunt Esther was in her thirties before the opportunity presented itself to acquire a building just downhill from 12 Cliff Road.

Cathcart's grocery store served the North Shore neighborhood, and seniors who grew up during the 1930s recall going there for penny candy. By the time of World War II, however, the days of Nantucket's family-run groceries were coming to an end. Harry Cathcart, a classmate of Esther's in school, had died while away at college, and his family was ready to close out their business.

Esther's savings wouldn't cover the down payment and the start-up costs, however, and the local bank refused her a loan on the grounds that she had no father or husband to back her enterprise. Instead, Centre Street businesswoman Cora Stevens extended an interest-free loan, and Esther was able to go forward with her plans.

With experience gained working in other restaurants and the goodwill of Cora Stevens and the Cathcarts, Esther set to work converting the store into a dining room and kitchen. In the summer of 1943 she had her own common victualler's license and was in business. The name of her restaurant was the North Shore.

To begin with, Esther's brother, Uncle John, was the restaurant's pastry chef. He had taken up where Grampa Gibbs left off, specializing in pies — in particular mince pie.

Wartime was an inauspicious moment to open a restaurant. In an era of meat points and one-pound sugar allotments, it took ingenuity to work around scarcity. Some of the practices from that time became permanent at the North Shore. In Aunt Esther's kitchen no one ever broke an egg directly into a mixing bowl. Each egg was broken into a cup and inspected before being added to other ingredients. Circumstances forced reliance on locally produced eggs, fish, fruit, and vegetables long before the word *locavore* was invented.

Many people of means who would otherwise have gone to Europe on vacation instead spent their wartime summers on Nantucket. For those staying in the neighborhood's hotels and guesthouses, the North Shore was one of the few available choices, and some people dined there every day of their stay. The dining room opened for dinner at 5:30 and orders were taken until eight. Reservations were not taken, and there was no bar. Customers came to sit on the benches outside an hour before opening time, and sometimes the line of customers waiting on the sidewalk rounded the corner from Centre Street onto Lily Street.

In the postwar years, despite growing competition from new restaurants opening on the island, the North Shore's popularity continued. In peacetime as in wartime, the drawing card for the North Shore was its off-the-boat seafood, produce from local farms, and homey desserts. Preparations were simple; freshness was all. The North Shore's longtime advertising slogan was "For excellent food reasonably priced."

A 1958 price list for North Shore menu items shows mainly traditional New England dishes with some Scandinavian and Floridian ones. Aunt Esther's key lime pie was a favorite of customers and staff alike, although at the end of service there was rarely a slice left for the staff to share.

The first two decades of my life were lived in and around the North Shore Restaurant. A very early memory is of sitting on the edge of an excavation with my feet dangling over as Aunt Esther and Uncle John dug a huge foundation hole. After a few summers of cooking from a tiny kitchen, they had decided to extend it back over a new storage cellar. In the end, the North Shore was unique among Nantucket restaurants in having a kitchen larger than its dining room.

It seems that just about every girl cousin, niece, in-law, and neighbor's daughter (not to mention college girls from out of state) did a stint of waiting on table at the North Shore. Aunt Esther was an exacting boss, and she had a rule that to be a waitress in her restaurant, one had to be at least eighteen years old and to have finished one year of college.

The rule was not bent for family members, so I spent my high school summers making sandwiches, salads, and "fresh fruit floats" at Reginald Haskell's Rainbow Put-up Lunch. It was a less pressured environment than the restaurant, and I was rewarded with incremental raises for learning my job and doing it well.

The summer I was eighteen, college still lay before me in the fall. I could not yet begin working at the North Shore, and I had outgrown the sandwich shop, so I worked that summer for the *Inquirer and Mirror* as proofreader, sometimes writer, and general help in the print shop, where my brother Tony ran the press.

The next summer I could at last earn real money as a waitress. At staff supper before dinner service began, we were fed from the menu so we could describe the entrées to the customers. Knowing the menu and being able to tell customers about the food with genuine enthusiasm earned good tips. When I returned to college in the fall, my savings were such that my dean gasped and asked, "Oh my dear, what did you do?"

I had crushes on the dishwashers, most of whom seem to have come to Nantucket from the Yale Drama School. They gave me paperback editions of existentialist literature, but otherwise didn't take my mooning after them seriously.

They had to take Aunt Esther seriously; she was intimidating on the job. Over time most of her employees came to appreciate her fairness and her kind side, however, and they would come back to work at the North Shore for several years running. For her fiftieth birthday the dishwashers, the waitresses (including me), and the cashier all went in on buying her a little model ship discovered in a local antique store. On the ship's transom was painted: *Pera, Finland*. I wonder if it was a joke on the part of the model-maker, since *perä* with dots over the *a* means "stern" in Finnish.

Aunt Esther did all the cooking at the North Shore, without benefit of a *sous chef*, so there was no reason for her to write down her restaurant recipes and file them in the boxes I inherited. Things were done without reference to books or note cards.

Quahog chowder base by the gallon was mixed with cream and gently warmed for serving each evening. For the chowder, there was a rule: the quahogs must be chopped with a knife, never ground in a meat grinder.

Potatoes, too, were handled with care. Every afternoon the college boys who ran the dishwasher and mopped the floors also peeled potatoes for the chowder and for the french fries, which were cut to order by a mechanical cutter that took in whole potatoes and pushed out uniform pieces for the fry baskets.

Cooked lobsters to be stuffed and run under the broiler were split with a cleaver, until one evening during dinner service there was a bloody accident. After that, Aunt Esther acquired a heavy aluminum restaurant-grade lobster splitter that we called the lobster guillotine. Eventually, along with the boxes of recipes, I inherited the guillotine, which I disposed of at a yard sale.

The one recipe that did come to me from the restaurant was for one of the North Shore's signature desserts.

ESTHER'S FROMAGE PIE

Preheat oven to 350°
Prepare a graham cracker crust in a deep ten-inch pie plate.
Beat together:
1 pound of cream cheese
3 eggs
1/2 cup sugar
1 teaspoon of vanilla
When smooth, pour into the piecrust and bake for twenty minutes.

While the filling is baking, blend together without stirring too much:
1/2 pint of sour cream
1/3 cup sugar
A dash of vanilla

Remove the pie from the oven and turn the temperature up to 450°.
Spread the sour cream mixture evenly over the pie, return to the oven, and bake for five minutes.

The product of this recipe resembles the difficult "feely" soured milk of Finland in that a bright white topping covers a more solid filling, but there is a world of difference in taste and texture.

For Easter at home Aunt Esther made an equally rich dessert called *paskha,* a molded uncooked cheesecake that came to Finland through the

Russian Orthodox Church and has become thoroughly naturalized, even in Finnish Lutheran homes. Craftsmen carve wooden paskha molds to sell in the markets, and back in the 1980s I was given one as a present at the end of the teaching year. In lieu of a paskha mold, a new terra cotta flowerpot can be used, but Aunt Esther had a different substitute. She used her *chinoise* (a sieve used to strain soups and sauces) to create a tall cone. Whatever one uses to mold the paskha, it must have a hole or holes to allow whey to drain out.

There are as many paskha recipes as families that make it. Many call for farmer cheese, Russian cottage cheese (*tvorog*), or Finnish *maitorahka*, none of which are readily available. I have made it with ricotta and also with large-curd cottage cheese forced through a food mill. This recipe of Esther's has the advantage of simplicity and does not include uncooked egg yolks as many recipes do.

ESTHER'S PASKHA

1/2 cup sour cream
3/4 pound cream cheese
1/4 pound unsalted butter
1/2 cup sugar
1 cup finely chopped almonds
1/2 cup mixed candied citron
1 1/2 cup seedless raisins
1 envelope plain gelatin
1/2 cup cold water

Soften gelatin in cold water. Cook in double boiler over hot water until completely dissolved.
Cream together cream cheese, butter, sour cream, and sugar until very smooth. Add almonds, citron, and raisins.

Add gelatin.
Mix well and pour into 4-cup mold lined with dampened cheesecloth.
Set on a dish to catch whey and refrigerate overnight.
Unmold on a serving plate and decorate with glazed cherries or flowers.

With paskha it is traditional to serve a delicate sweet bread called *kulich*. The kulich is baked in coffee cans from which the bread puffs out at the top in domes. Several kulich loaves surrounding a spire of paskha resembles an Orthodox church.

Miss Ellen Ramsdell lived halfway between 12 Cliff Road at the top of the hill and the North Shore Restaurant at the bottom of the hill. She operated a gift shop and also had a mail-order service. Along with garden-oriented gifts, Ellen sold jams, jellies, relishes, and fudge. When the North Shore closed each year shortly after Labor Day, Esther would make fudge for Ellen's business. Ellen kept careful records of the recipes and annotated them.

ESTHER'S CHOCOLATE FUDGE (1960. Best yet.)

6 cups sugar
2 cups evaporated milk
1 1/2 cup fudge base
Pinch salt
2 tablespoons Karo Syrup
Stir until all ingredients are well mixed.
Let boil until a soft ball forms in cold water.
Remove from heat.
Add stick of butter.
Let stand until butter is melted.
Add vanilla and 1 large cooking spoon of fondant.
Add nut meats.   *(Yield 6 pounds)*

Fudge base is a commercially available blend of cacao powder, butter, vanilla, and other ingredients. Fondant is also commercially available.

When my Finnish mother-in-law visited Nantucket in the 1970s, Esther went all out to impress her. We stayed at 12 Cliff Road, and Esther served us a splendid dinner there. We began with daiquiris in the front room, and then we moved to the dining room for bay scallops broiled in lemon butter with white wine. For dessert we had Esther's key lime pie. The food was unfamiliar to my mother-in-law, and I am not sure she enjoyed it, but she was impressed by the setting and the presentation. As for me, that meal was so perfect that I felt I couldn't bear to spoil it by ever eating again. Morning inevitably came and with it breakfast, but the memory remains indelible.

When Esther retired from operating the North Shore, she ran for a position on the Nantucket Board of Selectmen on the platform of No Re-election. Each and every decision, she promised, would be based on merit with no concern for whether it would keep her from being elected to another term. Her first term was so successful that she was re-elected handily. Unmarried and childless, she liked to refer to herself as the Town Mother.

Back when I was in high school, Aunt Esther had given me a typewriter and told me to write. During most of her lifetime, the academic books and articles I published were a disappointment to her. As her health began to fail in her eighties, I hurried to write a book of stories just for her with the title *Between Worlds*. It is about people who have heroically straddled two worlds, people like her own mother. She read it chapter by chapter as I wrote them, and it was done in time for her to see the dedication to Esther Ulrika Gibbs.

58

Ellen Ramsdell (1898–1991)
riding her bicycle down North Centre Street in 1922.
The cobblestones had been covered with asphalt just the year before.

Chapter 8
Miss Ramsdell

Unlike my several Cousins Ellen, Ellen Ramsdell was not named in memory of Gram's sister. Her mother was from an Azorean immigrant family, the Sylvaros, and her father was one of the Madaket Ramsdells — Warren's Landing on Madaket Harbor having been named for Ellen's paternal grandfather, Warren Ramsdell.

A 1917 graduate of the Coffin School (*Admiral Sir Isaac Coffin's Lancasterian School, founded 1827, Since 1903 Devoted to the Practical Arts*) and then of the New England Conservatory, Miss Ramsdell was music teacher to us all. The Nantucket public schools hired her as Supervisor of Music in 1930, and she continued in that capacity for nearly a quarter of a century.

She lived to the age of ninety-three, and for almost all of that time she was our family's close-by neighbor.

In 1869, Ellen's grandparents, Enos and Ellen Sylvaro, acquired the house at 67 North Centre Street, halfway between the intersection with Cliff Road at the top of the hill and the intersection with West Chester Street at the foot of the hill. Apparently it took a middleman to make the purchase. A member of the Swain family bought the property from the Widow Myrick and then sold it to the Sylvaros.

In the tiny house the Sylvaros raised a family of six children. At the time, there was only a small "borning room" off the front room downstairs and a sleeping loft with a fireplace upstairs. When I once asked how Mrs. Sylvaro managed, I was told that people slept in every room, and everyone was encouraged to get up, dressed, and out early in the morning. A photograph from the 1890s shows an unusual privy behind the house. Unlike most cold, dark privies, it had windows and a stovepipe, perhaps to make up for the cramped quarters of the house.

Sons Ferdinand and Emerson Sylvaro followed their father, Captain Enos Sylvaro, into a life on the water. The two brothers owned catboats that they used for fishing in the winter and taking visitors day-sailing in the summer. Ferdinand also had a painting business and became a master basket maker whose lightship baskets are now collector's pieces. His younger brother, Emerson, never left home.

Sisters Josephine and Edith died young, and Leonora married and moved to Boston.

Lizzie Sylvaro Ramsdell and Edgar Ramsdell with baby Ellen at Warren's Landing in 1899.

Their remaining sister, Elizabeth "Lizzie" Sylvaro, married Edgar Ramsdell and moved to the Ramsdell farm in Madaket, where baby Ellen was born in 1898. Less than four years later, after Edgar's small boat was swept out to sea through the opening between Smith's Point and Tuckernuck, his young widow took her little daughter Ellen back home to North Centre Street.

Two years after Lizzie's tragic homecoming, Enos Sylvaro died. Ferdinand had married and established his own home on Orange Street, so little Ellen grew up with her grandmother, her mother, and her Uncle Emerson. Then Lizzie died suddenly, and two years later Ellen's grandmother, Ellen Sylvaro, died as well, leaving Ellen and Emerson to share the family homestead.

In several ways, Ellen Ramsdell's life mirrored that of the Gibbs family up the hill. Like Grampa Gibbs, Ellen grew up without brothers and sisters in a fatherless household. Like the Gibbs children, she lost a parent without warning before she was quite prepared for life on her own. And while the Gibbs children lived a fusion of Old Nantucket and Finnish heritage, Ellen's experience was a fusion of Old Nantucket and Portuguese heritage. In culinary terms it might be characterized as chowder versus pickled herring at the top of the hill and chowder versus kale soup halfway down the hill.

Along with onions, tomatoes, and garlic, the kale would have come from the Sylvaros' own garden. Wherever Azorean immigrants have gone, they have created abundantly productive gardens around their homes, no matter how little land they have had to work with. When I first saw *Urban Cottage Gardens of the Portuguese Community*, a documentary produced by Spinner Publications of New Bedford, I recognized at once the garden Ellen inherited and tended throughout her life.

62

The grape arbor was a late addition, but Ellen's notebooks and her garden stakes — some weathered almost to illegibility — show that she maintained a vegetable garden with tomatoes, basil, peppers, parsley, thyme, peas, carrots, and beets. There were also strawberries. Once she became mistress of the house at 67 North Centre Street, she replaced the old wooden fence with a sculptured privet hedge and filled front and side yards with flowers: ageratum, bleeding hearts, calendulas, campanulas, dahlias, daisies, delphiniums, lilies, gladiolas, hydrangeas, marigolds, pinks, scabiosa, snapdragons, and a multitude of roses. The little house with its exuberant gardens became a stop on walking tours of the town.

Ellen's investment in horticulture compensated for the sacrifice of many young dreams. For some reason, it had taken her an extra year to graduate from high school, and when she did so, it was from the Coffin School, where her uncles had gone, rather than from Nantucket High School. Finally free, she went to Boston to study music, capitalizing on her extraordinary contralto voice. At the New England Conservatory, she qualified in both piano and organ as well. There were plans for a European tour and a concert career. She bought an elegant gown for her public appearances.

Right through 1921, photos show a happy, self-assured young woman with a crowd of young friends enjoying summer days at the beach and out sailing. She still has a joyous look about her in photos taken during the summer of 1922, although her mother had died on the last day of 1921.

Bit by bit through the 1920s, however, visions of the future narrowed. Ellen taught music in Maine and in Connecticut. The beautiful gown for concert appearances went into storage. The European tour was put on hold. She turned down a marriage proposal.

The stock market crash of 1929 and the coming of the Great Depression brought ambition to a standstill. In the fall of 1930, Ellen began teaching in the Nantucket public schools. She was appointed as Supervisor of Music, but she also had to teach fifth grade for no additional compensation. In the Nantucket annual town report, hope was expressed that at some time in the future she would be relieved of responsibility for the fifth grade and be able to devote herself full time to supervising music.

Bringing to the school music program the same passion she brought to gardening, Ellen directed young students, many still in elementary school, in demanding productions of Gilbert and Sullivan's *Pinafore*, *The Pirates of Penzance*, and *The Mikado*, as well as other musicals and a play-and-music festival.

On stage at the Cyrus Peirce School: cast of The HMS Pinafore, *directed by Ellen Ramsdell in 1938*

To augment her school salary, she became organist and choir director at St. Paul's Episcopal Church and accompanist for musicians visiting from the mainland. From time to time, she would sing a program herself, dressed in her elegant 1920s gown.

She might have completed a full quarter century as Supervisor of Music in the schools, had she not begun to go deaf. Anticipating retirement, she had a small cottage built in her garden and opened The Garden Gate gift shop. Her Uncle Emerson made the sign for her new business.

In June 1952, she advertised "unusual and useful" gifts, imports, hand-blown glass, and figurines. The Garden Gate also offered plants and fudge. For the off-season she opened a mail-order line of preserves. On her price list were seventeen jams and jellies, seven relishes and chutneys, and jars of mincemeat. "All are home-made in small quantities," Ellen assured her customers, with no artificial pectin and with "only the best grade of imported spices." At the bottom of the list were "Home-made Fudge and Penuche." Christmas orders would be packed with native greens and berries.

Annotated recipes for thirteen of the items on the price list are among those left to me, along with recipes for another twelve items (jams, marmalades, chutneys, and relishes) that do not appear on this particular list.

Since how to make them was common knowledge on the island, there are no recipe cards for jellies and jams made from beach plums, grapes, and blackberries.

Rose hip jam has only three ingredients, but preparation is not so simple, and Ellen had a card for it:

ROSE HIP JAM

Cut off hulls from rose hips and remove fuzz inside.
Wash thoroughly.
Cover with water, and let boil until soft.
Put through fine sieve.
To each cup of purée add 1 cup sugar.
Boil until thickened.
Fill hot jars and cover with paraffin.

Combining cranberries with pineapple, onion, and spices was innovative and complex. It rated not only written instructions, but the annotation "Excellent."

NANTUCKET CRANBERRY-PINEAPPLE CHUTNEY

1/2 cup water
4 cups cranberries
1 cup raisins
2 cups sugar
1/2 teaspoon each ginger and cinnamon
1/4 teaspoon allspice
1/4 teaspoon salt
dash of cayenne pepper
1 #2 can of pineapple chunks, drained
1 medium-sized onion sliced thin
Combine water, cranberries, raisins, sugar, and spices.
Mix well and cook over moderate heat until cranberries pop and mixture starts to thicken, about twenty minutes.
Stir in the drained pineapple chunks and onion slices.
Continue cooking another twenty minutes until mixture is thick as desired.
Makes four eight-ounce jars.

Note: I used crushed pineapple in a batch and it was just as good if not better than chunks.
Made several batches in fall of '58 and it sold well.

There is a story behind one of the items on the price list; Aunt Esther created it in Ellen's kitchen during the blizzard on the eve of President Kennedy's inauguration. The next day someone photographed 67 North Centre Street in all the snow and gave a print of the photo to Esther and Ellen.

67 North Centre Street after the Inuaguration Day blizzard of 1961

SIX FRUIT MARMALADE
(Concocted by Es. in the blizzard of January 1961)

2 grapefruit
2 lemons
4 small oranges
1 1/2 quart cranberries
7 cups dried apricots
4 cups date nuggets
Slice fruit very thin.
Dissolve 20 cups of sugar in 10 cups of water and soak fruit in it overnight. Cook until thick.
(If you want the cranberries to remain whole, reserve them and then add them during the last hour of cooking.)

Most of Ellen's recipes indicate how many jars or pounds each recipe will yield, but there is no indication for this one. It was clearly a success, nonetheless, since Ellen included it in her mail-order items. The story of its creation dates the mailing list to no earlier than 1961, probably autumn of that year.

Here is the Garden Gate penuche recipe:

RICH ROYAL PENUCHE

6 cups light brown sugar
1/4 teaspoon salt
1 1/2 cup evaporated milk
1/2 cup water
Boil together until a soft ball is formed in cold water.
Stir constantly until it starts to boil, then occasionally to prevent burning.
Add 6 tablespoons butter.

68

Let stand until the butter melts, then beat.
Add vanilla and nut meats.
Yield: 2 1/2 pounds.

And in Esther's handwriting:

DIVINITY FUDGE

2 cups sugar
1/2 cup Karo Syrup
1/2 cup water
Stir together, cover, and heat.
When it boils, take off the cover.
Boil slowly until it forms 2 or 3 long threads.
Beat one egg white.
Add syrup mixture to egg white, beating constantly.
Add 3/4 cup nutmeats, 1/4 teaspoon salt, and 1 teaspoon vanilla.
Beat until it stands up.
Put in pan, cool, and cut in squares.

Ellen and Aunt Esther were working together year-round by the end of the 1950s. During the summers Ellen was evening cashier at the North Shore Restaurant, and after the restaurant closed in the fall, she and Esther made the jams, jellies, relishes, and fudge for the Garden Gate business.

They also traveled together in the off-season, sampling the cuisines of Mexico, the Caribbean, and Portugal. In 1968 they celebrated Ellen's seventieth birthday by embarking on her long-postponed grand tour of Europe and spending two whole months exploring England, Ireland, and the Continent.

Passport photos of Esther and Ellen

After Gram's and Uncle Emerson's deaths in the 1960s, Esther and Ellen combined households at 67 North Centre and lived together for the rest of their lives. Esther outlived Ellen by just a bit, and the two women left me the house and the recipes.

If people are laid to rest with kin, then — without benefit of marriage — our two families have been united in Prospect Hill Cemetery. Gram was the last to be buried in the crowded family plot in New North Cemetery. Ellen's mother and grandmother joined Enos, Josephine, and Edith in Newtown Cemetery. A different place had to be found for the next generation, so in a single plot at Prospect Hill lie Cousin Betty's father and stepmother, my parents, Emerson Sylvaro, Ellen Ramsdell, and Aunt Esther. The two women are buried side by side with matching headstones — Esther's with a garland of flowers and Ellen's with a musical chord. Ellen was buried in her concert gown.

*Captain Robert Edward Ruley and Mary Louise McLean
on their wedding day, September 25, 1952*

Chapter 9
Brother Bob

My brother, Robert Ruley, was born in 1924. Many people who know us are hard put to think of Bob and me as brother and sister, since we were born eighteen years apart and never lived together under the same roof. Bob had joined the Navy right out of high school and was serving in World War II when I came into the world.

For part of his time in the Navy Bob was stationed at Guantanamo Bay Naval Base at the far southeastern tip of Cuba. By the 1940s, the base — established at the end of the Spanish-American War — was already a half-century old, occupying land around the bay on which the U.S.A. held (and still holds) a perpetual lease.

Bob took to Cuba with enthusiasm. He kept a horse off-base and spent leave time exploring the mountainous backcountry on horseback. In later years, he enjoyed sport fishing in Cuban waters and time ashore in Havana. All of this ended with the Cuban Revolution of 1959. Bob managed to stay in Cuba a little longer, until the fall of 1960 when he was told in no uncertain terms that he had to leave on the next flight out and never come back.

At the time, I was a freshman in college, and Bob called me from Logan Airport to ask me to come join him while he waited for his connecting flight home to Nantucket. I drank ginger ale and he drank something stronger as we sat together in an airport bar that night. Bob was pale and shaken. I got the impression he had been put onto the plane in Cuba at gunpoint. I think this was the closest we ever approached each other. In retrospect, it seems odd that despite his attachment to Cuba, I never heard him speak a word of Spanish.

Before his discharge from the Navy, there had been another abrupt, life-altering event. On board ship, he and another sailor were moving a torpedo when it detonated, killing the other sailor and leaving my brother desperately injured. He was transported to the Charleston Naval Hospital, and our parents were notified by telegram that his chances of survival were slim. They put me into Gram's care and left immediately for South Carolina.

Cousin Ellen Gibbs wrote in her memoir of World War II:

> *Quite a few local boys were killed or hurt. One of my favorite*
> *cousins was hurt badly. I cried and prayed for him to recover*
> *so he could come home and tease me and try to steal a kiss like*
> *he used to. He was luckier than lots of other men. When the*
> *torpedo blew up, it killed the other man instantly, but Bob was*
> *a big fellow, and because of it he pulled through.*

Against the odds he did survive, but he carried deep scars and needles of shrapnel in his body for the rest of his life. Discharged from the Navy, he was admitted to Brown University, but in cold weather his lungs began to bleed. It was evident that he could not spend winters in Rhode Island, so he withdrew from college and went back to life on the Caribbean as captain of various sorts of vessels.

Even after he married and began a family, fall would take him away from Nantucket to the warm waters of South Florida, the Bahamas, and—as long as he was permitted to stay on—to Cuba. He would get there early enough in the fall that when the annual migration of monarch butterflies passed over the Caribbean, they would settle all over his boat to rest before moving on. His descriptions of the clarity of the deep blue water, allowing vision down to spectacular depths, were breathtaking for those of us back at home.

When Aunt Esther decided to retire from running the North Shore Restaurant, she made a trip to Florida to meet with Bob and offer the restaurant business to him and his wife, Mary Louise. Their growing children needed their father at home, she said, and after so many years of healing, perhaps his lungs could tolerate the island's winter cold.

Although he had a healthy appetite and our father's appreciation of good quality, I had never thought of Brother Bob as a foodie. Mary Lou's mother had been with the North Shore Restaurant from its inception, however, and like so many of us, Mary Lou had waited on table there in the summers. There was no mystery to the operation of the restaurant, and the transition from Esther Gibbs to Bob and Mary Lou Ruley was to all appearances seamless.

The Ruley children, six in all, got their first work experience helping out in their parents' restaurant. The clientele of the North Shore were so faithful over so many years that my nieces and I could compare notes about serving the self-same customers, such as the solitary Russian émigré who would make a point of ordering dinner without potatoes and then roar, "No potatoes!" as his waitress emerged from the kitchen with his entrée. Or the pair of academic brothers who might have been models for television's Frasier and Niles Crane, both of them resembling delicate Niles more than robust Frasier. Or the portly couple who, at least once a week, would take a window table for four and tie it up for hours. Or the poor lady who fell out of her chair so regularly that whichever waitress was closest would help her up while hardly breaking stride.

Bit by bit the menu and the operation evolved under the new management, and Aunt Esther found it difficult to observe from the little house halfway up the hill where she and Ellen Ramsdell lived in retirement from their businesses. Hardest of all for Esther was when Bob and Mary Lou retired and sold the restaurant. The North Shore had been dear to many, and it was hard to bid it good-by. Esther told me that she had hoped that I might take it over, but it was not to be. She also advised me that if one truly enjoys food, one should stay out of the business, because the day-to-day stress spoils it. Still, she thought, it wouldn't be such a bad thing to do a little catering.

Chicken livers had never been on the menu at the North Shore, but every chicken purchased for the restaurant came with its liver in a bag tucked inside. The bags accumulated in the freezer until Bob decided that he had to invent a chicken liver dish that "even children will eat." It never went on the North Shore menu, but it was served for staff supper, and it has been a mainstay at my house since Bob told it to me one evening.

BROTHER BOB'S CHICKEN LIVERS

Sauté sliced mushrooms in butter.
Remove from pan and reserve.
Dredge chicken livers in flour, salt, and pepper.
Sauté the livers in the same pan as the mushrooms, adding butter as needed, until browned on all sides but not cooked through.
Remove livers from pan and reserve with the mushrooms.
Deglaze the pan with one cup of beef consommé.
Add one-quarter cup cooking sherry.
Cook until somewhat thickened.
Return mushrooms and livers to pan, cover and cook until the livers are done.
Just before serving, add a handful of chopped parsley.
Serve over steamed rice.

In telling me this recipe, Bob said, "There's no such thing as too much parsley." Mary Lou retorted, "Oh yes, there is."

When I serve Bob's chicken livers to guests, I offer along with them something a bit tart—either Gram's pickled cucumbers or cranberry sauce or lingonberries if we are fortunate enough to have them. Cranberry pepper jelly is also a good accompaniment.

These were the reciprocal gifts Brother Bob and I exchanged: I kept him company for an hour on a scary night in 1960, and he gave me a real keeper of a recipe.

Frances Ruley Karttunen in the classroom, 1989

Chapter 10
The Author

My earliest memory of cooking is of baking with Gram, but Mother and I cooked together often in the years before her health failed. We made jelly rolls, turning the sponge cake out onto a linen towel, cutting off the stiff edges, spreading it with jelly and then using the towel to gently roll it up.

Another cake involved using the hand-cranked flour sifter to mix the dry ingredients and, at the end, dripping melted chocolate over white frosting. The unsweetened chocolate finish was not to my taste, but grown-ups considered it a great treat. I was surprised to find the recipe in one of the boxes I inherited.

TAR ROOF CAKE

First bake a hot milk cake:

Preheat oven to 350°.
Beat 2 eggs thoroughly.
Add 1 cup sugar, beating it in a little at a time.
Add salt and vanilla.
Sift together 1cup flour with 1 teaspoon baking powder.
Add to the egg mixture and beat once more.
Heat 1/2 cup milk carefully.
Add a piece of butter the size of a walnut to the warm milk and let it melt.
Add to the other mixture and beat well.
Pour into greased and floured pan and bake for 30 minutes.

When cool, frost with butter-and-sugar frosting.

Melt unsweetened baker's chocolate in a double boiler and drip over the top of the frosted cake.
Let it set to make the tar roof.

This recipe as written makes enough batter to bake in one nine-inch round cake pan. To make a layer cake, double the recipe and bake in two nine-inch pans. I use cake flour in this recipe, but all-purpose flour works better for dusting the greased cake pans.

Mother was fearless in letting me make krom cakes (*krumkake* in Norwegian) with an iron over an open-flame burner and frying rosettes in deep fat with a timbal iron. The batters for both are simple, but the execution is tricky. I still have our krom iron after all these years, but the timbal iron with its rosette, butterfly, and star attachments seems to have gone its own way.

I made the crisp, delicate krom cakes and rosettes all through high school, college, and beyond for especially festive occasions. A quicker, easier treat was gingerbread. In the summers during my high school years, I helped at the weekly Maria Mitchell Observatory open nights and often took along a pan of fresh-baked gingerbread to share around after the public departed. These days the Ruley family Christmas Eve meal always concludes with warm gingerbread and clouds of whipped cream.

During high school I earned money toward college by doing seamstress work—making cheer-leader and majorette uniforms for girls in Nantucket High School, tailoring resort clothes for Aunt Esther's winter travels, and taking up countless hems as women's skirts shortened radically with the arrival of the 1960s. One of my clients was Ethel Anastos, who had come to Nantucket as a young bride and wanted curtains made for her new home on Union Street. I sewed the curtains for the Anastos house and came away with Greek recipes. One was for a chicken dish flavored with cinnamon. Another was for chicken-egg-lemon soup.

At college, there was no in-house Sunday evening meal, so almost every week we would go around to the Forest Café on Massachusetts Avenue for the cheapest possible supper of chicken-egg-lemon soup with chunks of fresh-baked bread. If we were really flush, we might have a Greek salad with feta cheese and olives along with the soup and bread. The café had a jukebox, and it was during one of those suppers that I heard the Beatles for the very first time. Ever since, I have associated *I Wanna Hold Your Hand* with this tangy, life-sustaining soup I first learned from Ethel Anastos.

CHICKEN-EGG-LEMON SOUP

Warm chicken broth (home-made if possible, and with a bit of rice in it).
Add fresh-squeezed lemon juice to the broth.
Beat an egg well and while still beating, pour some of the warm broth into the beaten egg.
Immediately pour the egg mixture into the rest of the broth, beating all the while to produce a velvety texture.
Garnish with a little chopped green onion.
Serve with bread chunks.

At college I lived in a cooperative house where we rotated in pairs making meals for the twenty-five residents. My housemate Susan tells much-embellished tales of our adventures in cooking. The running theme of her stories is hapless Susan and resourceful Fran — resourceful to the point of going out and shooting a duck on the Charles River to provide for the coop. In fact, I had brought ducks, dressed and frozen solid, back to Cambridge from Nantucket. For the one woman among us who refused to eat anything that had been shot out of the sky by Brother Bob and his hunting buddies, we bought a domestic duck at a local market.

Our coop shopped at the same market as Julia Child, and we sometimes were there at the same time. She would wave to us merrily, and we would do our best to emulate her in the coop kitchen, explaining to each other in high-pitched voices exactly how we were doing our preparations.

Susan's best story on herself is of being single-handedly responsible for dinner one day when she got last-minute news that a dean would be joining us on a coop inspection tour. Susan had made a pot of chili and planned to just ladle it out in the kitchen, but the dean rated a proper sit-down dinner and a green vegetable. What would Julia Child have done? Susan boiled up a package of frozen peas, set bowls of red chili on dinner plates, and arranged a circle of bright green peas around each bowl.

Many years later, my husband and I were invited to Julia Child's eightieth birthday celebration at the Smithsonian Museum of American History. It was a gala weekend with more meals than any mortal could hope to consume. To encourage our appetites, the movie theater in Georgetown was showing the film *Babette's Feast*.

During my undergraduate years in Cambridge I had never approached Julia, only smiled and waved. Now my daughter Jaana was about to finish her graduate degree in California. As a graduation present I had bought a canvas bag printed with the faces of grandmotherly women and the words "Many Strong and Beautiful Women" with the intention of filling it with cookbooks. Aunt Esther and Mary Lou had signed the bag, and so had other women in our family. At Julia's birthday celebration, I had it signed by Alice Waters, whose Chez Panisse restaurant was not far from where my daughter lived in Berkeley. I was feeling too shy to ask Julia for an autograph, but Alice Waters said, "Oh, go ahead. She's a pussycat." With her encouragement I dared, and in a bold hand Julia wrote across the back of the bag, "Bon Appétit! Julia Child."

When Jaana and her sister Suvi were growing up, we made many visits to Finland, often for months at a time. Finnish food was completely familiar, and I think we all took it for granted. Living on the edge of one of Finland's thousands of lakes on summer visits, we caught and cooked freshwater fish—perch, pike, and smelts. After sauna, like everyone else, we speared chunks of sausage, cooked them over an open fire, and ate them with sweet mustard. We introduced our Finnish friends to popcorn (a huge hit) and chili, which we sometimes made with reindeer meat (very stomach-warming was the verdict).

Back in Austin, Texas, where we lived when not in Finland, there were Finns and Friends picnics, spring and fall, where we enjoyed a great variety of Finnish food: meat and rice rolled up in cabbage leaves, rutabaga and carrot casseroles, beet salad, and other quintessential Scandinavian dishes. From time to time for these picnics I would try baking the kinds of bread we all missed, but despite the availability of rye flour, my results were never up to the standards of commercial bakeries.

Whether in Finland or in Austin, our at-home staples included cardamom braids, pancakes, meatballs, and pickled cucumbers. For parties I would serve homemade liver paté with lingonberries, little mushroom turnovers, and Finnish cheeses with crisp bread. In spring we would make a fizzy, hops-flavored May Day drink called *sima*, and at the start of the Christmas season I would make *glögg* — sweetened, and spiced warm red wine that is flamed just before serving.

Prior to one of Western Europe's calendar reforms, the winter solstice fell on December 13, which happened to be Saint Lucy's day on the church calendar. In Sweden, the day is celebrated as *Luciadag*, while in Finland it is known as Little Christmas. This is the official first day for enjoying glögg. In rural Finland, the absolute last day is January 13, when all remaining Christmas food and drink in the household must be consumed by midnight, and mummers travel house to house to help out.

There was never glögg in Gram's house. The first time I had it was on a bitterly cold December night in Cambridge, and like reindeer meat chili, it proved very stomach-warming.

There are many recipes, but basically glögg calls for a blend of sweet and dry red wines. The spices are so assertive that there is no point to subtlety in choice of wine. For a big party, I would ask guests to bring bottles of inexpensive red wine and try to balance dry with sweet.

GLÖGG

A few days in advance, have on hand a large glass jar for the base.

For each 2 bottles of wine you plan to add to the final product, put into a saucepan:
4 whole cloves
8 whole cardamoms
1/2 cup blanched/shredded almonds
1 cup raisins
A curl of orange peel
1 piece of stick cinnamon

Cover the fruit and spices with any kind of red wine, and bring to a simmer.
Let the mixture cool and pour it into the jar.
Cover tightly and refrigerate.

For the party, the wine needs to be kept warm without constant tending.
A large crockpot works well.

Put some of the base into the glögg pot.
Pour in equal parts of dry and sweet wine.
Bring to a simmer.
Put some sugar cubes in a long-handled strainer or slotted spoon.
Heat a small amount of vodka in a saucepan on the stove (very carefully). Have matches and a cover for the pot on hand.
Hold the strainer over the glögg and pour the warm vodka over the sugar cubes.
Strike a match, and pass it over the strainer.
(Alternatively, place a metal cake rack over the top of the pot, spread vodka soaked sugar cubes on it, and light them.)
Don't do this near curtains, and keep face and hair back, because the alcohol lights with a puff and then burns with such a pale blue flame that it may not be immediately noticeable.
If things seem to burn too fast or too long, cover the pot with its lid, and the flame will go out right away.
The burning vodka will melt the sugar, but not entirely.
Ladle hot glögg over what is left, and tip it in.
Melting the sugar gives the glögg a soft, caramel flavor, whereas if sugar is merely added without flaming, it tastes raw.

Glögg is a strong drink, so serve it in small cups or mugs, being sure each serving includes an almond and some raisins.

Leftover glögg can be reheated the next day, but it soon turns vinegary.

Over the years at the University of Texas, I received three Fulbright
Fellowships, all to Finland. On the other hand, support I received from
the National Endowment for the Humanities and the National Science
Foundation was all for work in and about indigenous Mexico. I compiled
a dictionary of Nahuatl, one of the major Indian languages of Mexico,
and created workbooks for teaching the language in summer courses.

I used cooking both to learn the language and to teach it. Living in an
Indian town in Mexico, I would sit with women on tiny chairs
resembling children's toys and make tortillas with them. We would take
turns plopping down a handful of soaked ground cornmeal known as
nixtamal onto a *metate*, a stone grinding table, and then we would work it
into a fine dough with a stone rolling pin known as a *metlapil*. (All these
special terms are Nahuatl words that have been borrowed into Spanish.)
Shaping the dough into small lumps, we would pat it between our palms
to make a flat disk and then give it a few spins before dropping it onto a
comal (griddle) over an open fire. The tortillas would puff like little
balloons, and we would flip them with our fingertips and then slide
them off the comal into a round basket.

My patting and spinning technique was flawed, producing oblong,
football-shaped tortillas that wouldn't fit into the basket, so we would
have to eat them on the spot. We would get so giddy with laughter that
we would fall off our little chairs, and eventually we would be too
stuffed to go on.

Beyond learning the names for the ingredients and utensils, I would ask
questions along the lines of: "What are we doing here?" "What did we
just do?" "What will we do next?" Bit by bit, I would learn how the verbs
worked in that particular community, how to talk about the past, the
present, and the immediate future. My cooking companions good-

naturedly showed me how to ask questions and how to understand answers.

A *tamale* is cornmeal dough wrapped around a filling, tied up in a cornhusk, and steamed. When teaching at universities, I would invite people learning the language to a *tamalada*, a party for making tamales by assembly line. One person pats the cornmeal dough onto a dampened cornhusk; the next person spreads on the filling, rolls it up, and passes it to another person who ties the ends; the last person arranges the tamales in the steaming pot. It's almost always a man who takes over that final step, warding off anyone else who might offer to lend a hand. As for tamale-tying, the most elegant work I've ever seen was done by a cardiologist.

In Texas, mass production of tamales goes on before Christmas, whereas in Mexico people make tamales by the hundreds for the Day of the Dead at the beginning of November. Whatever holiday is in the offing, people coming together at a tamalada enjoy each other's company and the sense of group accomplishment.

Traditional tamales are made with lard and *masa* (special Mexican cornmeal for tortillas and tamales now readily available in local grocery stores). I once took a bag of masa with me from Austin to Paris in order to make tamales for a party. There was no problem bringing the cornmeal into the country. As my French colleague remarked, it would never occur to French customs agents that anyone would bring food to France. Our problem was that we could not obtain lard. We spent most of an afternoon going from shop to shop asking, "Du lard?" and meeting with no success. Finally we settled for a solid vegetable shortening that worked quite well.

Lard makes tasty pie crust and tamale dough, but it isn't healthy for us.
What is more, some of the people I worked with were vegetarians. The
Austin farmers market sold tamales made with olive oil. It doesn't work
to simply replace a solid shortening with oil, however, and the vendors
were not willing to disclose their recipe. It took a while to get the
proportions of oil, cornmeal, and liquid right.

When I make tamales, I usually fill some with a mixture of ground pork,
raisins, and pine nuts; others with shredded chicken or turkey; others
with Monterrey jack cheese and canned green chiles; and some sweet
ones with cinnamon, brown sugar, and raisins. (Sweet tamales are
traditionally colored pink with a few drops of food coloring.)

These freeze wonderfully, and olive oil tamales seem to actually
improve by being steamed, frozen, and then re-steamed. I almost
always have several kinds in our freezer for when we need a quick
meal with minimum preparation.

TAMALES

Open a package of dried cornhusks for tamales and soak the husks in water.
When they are flexible, separate them and remove any corn silk still adhering to
them.
Tear some of the husks into narrow strips to use as ties.
Put wet husks into a large bowl covered with a towel so they don't dry out.

Prepare the dough.

Made with lard:
2/3 pound lard
4 cups masa
2 teaspoons salt

2 2/3 cups warm chicken or turkey broth

Add half of the warm broth and all the salt to the lard and work with a wooden spoon or hands until it is soft and light.
Gradually add masa, alternating with the rest of the broth.
Keep beating to make the mixture light and airy.
When it is ready, a little piece should float in a cup of cool water.

Made with olive oil:
3/4 cup olive oil
4 1/2 cups masa
2 teaspoons salt
2 1/2 cups warm chicken or turkey broth
(For vegetarian tamales, use vegetable broth.)

Put the olive oil and half the broth into the bowl of an electric mixer, using the paddle attachment. On slow speed, mix while gradually adding masa and salt alternating with broth. Keep mixing until dough is well formed. If the dough is too heavy for the mixer, add a little more liquid. This does not produce the airy batter that one can obtain by hand beating.

Spread a rectangle of the dough on a cornhusk, flush along one edge and stopping short of top and bottom. Place some filling on the rectangle, and then roll the husk around it. Tie both ends. The tamale will resemble a paper party cracker.

Arrange the tamales upright in a large steamer pot over an inch of water. Cover, bring the water to a boil, reduce to a simmer, and steam for 40 minutes.

President Gerald Ford, on a visit to San Antonio, Texas, famously tried to eat a tamale without unwrapping it. At a meal with tamales, there should be a large bowl in the middle of the table for disposal of the cornhusks. There should also be bowls of different kinds of salsa to go with the tamales.

Since the late 1980s my husband, Al Crosby, and I have been frequent visitors to the University of Hawaii. There is a significant Mexican collection in the library of the Oahu campus, and the curator of the collection and her husband became good friends. They are great fans of tamales and anticipate a tamalada whenever we visit. Fortunately, there is a Mexican market in Honolulu where we can buy masa.

We once spent a full academic year at the University of Hawaii, and I set about learning to cook with local ingredients. Like everyone else, I bought large bags of rice, and I steamed fish and vegetables in a multilevel steamer that came with our sublet apartment. We were almost the only non-Asians in our apartment tower, and from kitchens all around us came unfamiliar and sometimes unpleasant smells. I think the strangest ones must have been from fermentation. Sometimes we would roll up a beach towel and lay it against the threshold of our apartment door to try to keep the smell out. I imagine that our neighbors did not care for some of the aromas wafting from our kitchen either.

I never did take up cooking with tofu or Spam, but I quickly came to love and crave sweetened red adzuki beans with ice cream, tree-ripened mangoes, Hawaiian steamed dumplings called *manapua, huli huli* chicken hot and juicy from grills set up in parking lots on the weekends, and — from the student union cafeteria––lunchtime *bento* boxes with little pickled plums.

None of these did I learn to make for myself, but on Nantucket I achieved a bit of Hawaiian/New England fusion. Francina Reyes Gibbs, a cousin by marriage, operated a farm up-country on Maui. On a visit to Nantucket, she brought us the standard (and very much appreciated) hospitality gift from Hawaii, a large container of macadamia nuts. Together we went to the old Reyes family house on York Street where there was still a flourishing rhubarb patch planted by Cina's mother long ago. We cut an armload of the big red stalks, and from them I made this dessert.

RHUBARB-MACADAMIA CRISP

Heat oven to 375°.
Butter an 8-inch square baking dish.
Wash, trim, and coarsely chop rhubarb stalks.
Dissolve 1 tablespoon cornstarch in 3 tablespoons orange juice.
Toss 4 cups of chopped rhubarb with the orange juice mixture and 1 cup sugar.
Put fruit in baking dish and dot with little pieces of butter.
Mix 1/4 cup butter with 1/3 cup brown sugar, 2/3 cup flour, and 1/4 teaspoon salt.
Add lots of chopped macadamia nuts.
Spread topping over the fruit and bake for 40 minutes.
Serve warm with vanilla ice cream.

Frances Karttunen and Francina Reyes Gibbs
aboard the Sea Chanty *in 1987*

Most professional linguists I know are also food enthusiasts. It must have something to do with orality. They master the languages of far-flung places and also the cuisines. Although Aunt Esther was right that academic training had rendered me unavailable to take over the North Shore Restaurant, in some corner of my being I always yearned to be part of a small restaurant operation. I conceived of a linguistic restaurant called Mother Tongue where my colleagues and I would rotate different ethnic dishes from night to night, with tongue in various preparations the constant on the menu. Absolutely no one I ever talked with about it shared my vision.

Alfred W. Crosby

Chapter 11
Big Al

My husband brought to our marriage a collection of personae: Guido Boccigalupe, the Fixer; Alfredo de la Cruz, Tango King of the Baltic; and Big Al from Revere. Al actually grew up in suburban Boston — in Wellesley and, as he puts it, all of the Newtons. To my knowledge, he's never set foot in Revere, but Big Al from Revere sounds a whole lot more imposing than Al from Wellesley.

We met over *kir* and paté of thrush, and Al went on to court me with cheese scrambled eggs.

It began with Carlota, a colleague in the linguistics department at the University of Texas, and Marc from IBM France. Marc was coming to Austin for a conference I had organized, and he asked what he should bring with him. Carlota suggested a bottle of *crème de cassis* (black currant liqueur) for making kir (a white wine cocktail) and "some paté to go with it." Marc misunderstood and, thinking that some particular type of paté was the proper accompaniment for kir, he spent as much futile time in Paris shops asking about it as we once spent seeking lard. In the end, Marc simply brought a valise packed with a variety of little cans of paté, hoping not to embarrass himself by failing to bring the right one. The paté of thrush came with a little beak and claws pressed into the top, which was a bit unnerving.

For the post-conference party at her house, Carlota bought baguettes to go with the several patés and champagne to mix with the crème de cassis to make kir. It was at that party that I met Al.

Al was famous for his book, *The Columbian Exchange: Biological and Cultural Consequences of 1492*, which had grown out of an article of his,

"Conquista y Pestilencia," about the role of disease in the collapse of the Aztec empire. As we sipped kir and chatted, it was clear we shared many academic interests.

Mutual friend Carlota took it into her head to play matchmaker, and so annoyed both of us that we avoided each other for months until Carlota left Austin on vacation. As we got to know each other in her absence, we realized that she had been absolutely right about our compatibility.

My difficult sixteen-year marriage had collapsed irrevocably, and during the months that Al and I avoided each other, I was working with an attorney to dissolve it. Al, I learned, had come to the end of a marriage that had also endured for sixteen years despite problems that ultimately proved insuperable. From his perspective of several post-divorce years, he assured me that I would survive, no matter how awful I was currently feeling. One thing was clear to us; we both so believed in matrimony that we had each struggled for many years to preserve our former marriages. We were not quitters.

My daughters and I invited Al to join us for fried oysters on Christmas Day. For dessert we made *bûche de noël*, a chocolate sponge roll filled with hazel-nut cream. Instead of going to the trouble of making little meringue mushrooms to stick on and around it in the traditional French fashion, we decorated it with maraschino cherries. As it turns out, Al dislikes cherries in all forms, but he kindly did not say so that day. Instead he took note of the presentation, praising our "pretty food." By contrast he recalled a Thanksgiving meal from his boyhood that was so unattractive that he had not been able to hold his tongue, complaining that what was on his plate looked "like a dog's foot."

Al lived close to Suvi's middle school, and in the spring he began inviting Suvi and me to breakfast before school. He served us scrambled eggs, daringly mixing bleu cheese into them— something I never would have thought of.

Austin is full of pleasant, inexpensive cafés, and we frequented about a dozen of them. One we especially liked was a Caribbean restaurant called Tortuga's. Another was a combination restaurant and Swedish bakery. On weekend mornings we would walk from West Austin three miles downtown for a Mexican breakfast and three miles back to hike off the black beans, eggs, salsa, and tortillas.

It was evident that not only did we share a notion of what a happy marriage should be, we were united in appreciation of good food.

Al proposed to me at Tom's Tabooley, a Texas-Lebanese lunch spot. We had been sharing a plate of grape leaves stuffed with lemon-flavored rice and meat, our fingers dripping with olive oil. It was just as well Al did not offer an engagement ring, because we both would have had to excuse ourselves to go wash our hands before he could continue. Instead, he had brought along a large antique Afghan pendant that he asked me to accept without obligation. It took several tries to find a way to wear it comfortably, but now it has had many outings and once was nearly confiscated by airport security because it appeared so odd in the baggage scan. In the meantime, its country of origin has suffered so much that these days I feel equivocal about wearing it.

Al with Fran wearing the Afghan pendant

When we inherited the house at 67 North Centre Street, we also inherited the grapevines Aunt Esther and Ellen had planted decades earlier. In early summer the vines put out runners covered with tender young grape leaves. Then I make stuffed grape leaves in celebration of the day Al proposed.

STUFFED GRAPE LEAVES

Filling:
Brown a mixture of ground lamb and ground beef with a finely chopped shallot.
Flavor with salt, pepper, and cumin, tumeric, mint, or some combination.
Add cooked rice to the mixture.
Cover and cook over low heat for a while.
Turn off heat, and squeeze a lemon over the meat/rice mixture.
Refrigerate overnight to let the flavors merge.

Pick two or three dozen young grape leaves.
With kitchen scissors snip out the tough central rib.
Blanche leaves three or four at a time in simmering water.
Drain the leaves and let them cool.

Put a spoonful of filling on a prepared leaf.
Turn in the sides over the filling and roll up the filling in the leaf.
Put on a tray and keep filling leaves until the filling or the leaves run out.
Place the stuffed grape leaves in a steamer and steam for 30 minutes.

Pour some good olive oil over the stuffed grape leaves.

These are equally good hot or cold served with a sauce of sesame tahini whirled in a blender with water, garlic, salt, and lemon juice.

On a May day, Al and I were married in a judge's chambers in the company of our daughters. On inspiration, Suvi asked the clerk to dump out the reservoir of the office hole-punch machine, producing instant confetti. Then, in a rented Lincoln Town Car (the national car of Texas, according to Al), we all repaired to Tortuga's for a wedding lunch.

Soon after, Al had business in Boston, and from there we came on to
Nantucket to introduce him to my relatives. Years earlier, Aunt Esther
had provided a memorable dinner for my late mother-in-law. This time
she hosted a dinner memorable for what was said rather than for what
was served. When we were seated at her dining room table, she turned
to Al and asked in a skeptical tone of voice, "And what is it you say you
do for a living?" Without missing a beat, Al replied, "I live off women."
I had never seen Aunt Esther at a loss for words, but that evening we
dined in perfect silence.

As a rule Esther had a poor opinion of men; after all, it was men at the
bank who denied her a small-business loan on the grounds that she did
not have a husband to be responsible for her finances. She admired quick
wits and deadpan humor, however, and she made an exception for Al.
They became friends, and she was content that after she and Ellen died,
Al and I would live in the house and take care of it.

Al and I spent our second and third wedding anniversaries in Finland
with back-to-back Fulbright fellowships, plunging Al into the world of
moose meatballs, stringy yogurt, and polar cocktails (cranberry liqueur
and vodka on crushed ice). Al rarely met a Finnish cheese or pastry he
didn't love at first taste. He was particularly fond of the warm sugared
jelly doughnuts called *possuja* ("piglets") that are sold in the tent cafés
on Helsinki's market square. I like them, too, but became cautious about
eating them outdoors after a passing gull smacked the side of my head
with its wing, snatched my doughnut from my hand, and made off with
it.

Whether at home in Austin or away, Al would take his turn cooking by
making a one-dish meal he calls pork chop surprise (or, depending on
the ingredients at hand, sausage surprise). For us this has become a

regular fallback meal to be concocted with what is at hand in the pantry, refrigerator, and freezer.

AL'S PORK CHOP SURPRISE

Sauté a small chopped onion in a bit of olive oil.
Brown several pork chops in the same pan.
Add a cup of chopped celery and 1/2 cup of uncooked rice.
When the rice is slightly browned, add a half can of diced tomatoes.
Throw in a handful of raisins (optional).
Squeeze a lemon over everything.
Add a little more water as necessary.
Cover and simmer for 25 minutes until the rice is done.

As 1992 approached, both of us were kept busy with event planning for the 500th anniversary of the arrival of Columbus at Hispaniola and all that came in his wake. Because of *The Columbian Exchange*, Al was in demand all over the map: Santa Fe one week, Santo Domingo the next. We went to Barcelona and saw where Columbus's ships were built, and then we were on hand when a replica of the *Santa Maria*, built in Barcelona, put in at Honolulu on a transpacific voyage to complete what Columbus set out to do. Our frequent-flier balances were impressive.

Also in recognition of his publications, Al was invited to Genoa, where we discovered that Christopher Columbus is not much honored in his birthplace. There is a statue of him at the railroad station, and a building known as the Columbus House stands on the site of an earlier building that belonged to the explorer's father. In Genoa's splendid maritime museum, Christopher Columbus has an alcove; in the museum gift shop Columbus t-shirts were not to be found. The local hero is Admiral

Andrea Doria, a hometown boy who expelled French occupiers from his city and eventually governed it. In the main entry hall of the maritime museum is a huge model of the ill-fated liner that bore his name and sank in deep waters off Nantucket in 1956.

Along the waterfront next to the Genoa maritime museum, men sit in the sun mending nets, and small fishing boats put in to sell their catch of the day to waiting customers. We weren't familiar with the various types of Mediterranean fish, but we enjoyed watching them being tossed off the boats into people's outstretched hands.

In the summer of 1992, I directed a summer institute that traveled from Austin to the University of the Americas in Cholula, Mexico. While we were in Cholula, Al was one of the speakers at a conference on *El encuentro de dos comidas* — the encounter of Spanish and indigenous Mexican cuisines — that was held in the nearby city of Puebla. There we enjoyed a Spanish dinner the first evening and a Mexican dinner the second. The large and proud Lebanese community in Puebla could not let this pass, so on the third day they put on an impressive Middle Eastern lunch in Puebla's Lebanese cultural center. When the hospitality and the expressions of gratitude were finally exhausted, we could hardly waddle.

Austin's 6th Street, lined with bars and entertainment venues, strives to emulate Bourbon Street in New Orleans. A musician acquaintance of ours worked as a waiter in a cool, air-conditioned oyster house there. Now and then at the end of a hot summer afternoon we would stop in for a dozen oysters apiece. The oyster house survived barely six months after our friend left for New York to further his musical career. In the meantime, Al had picked up an at-home approach to oysters.

AL'S OYSTER MELT

Put a loaf of French bread in the oven to get warm and crispy.
Take it out and wrap it loosely to keep it warm.
Turn the oven up to broil.
Butter the cups of a muffin tin.
In each cup place a large oyster.
On top of it place a slice of good cheddar cheese.
Broil until the cheese melts and gets slightly bubbly.
With the one you love, share the oysters straight out of the muffin tin with torn-off hunks of French bread accompanied by cold, dry champagne.

Do it all over again.

Guido and the gang recommend it.

Calder family monument in New North Cemetery

Chapter 12
Calder Cousins and Next-Door Neighbors

In 1952, Miss Elsie Calder came to Nantucket to visit the Calder family graves in New North Cemetery. Of Miss Elsie my relatives said that she was "the last of her line." At age ten, I was impressed by their hushed voices as they said this. What did it mean?

Elsie Calder, born in 1895, and her sister, born in 1899, were the great-granddaughters of Captain Robert Calder, and there were no boys in their generation. Elsie's sister had married and taken her husband's name. Elsie remained unmarried and would carry the Calder name with her to her grave.

And why were my mother, Aunt Esther, and I the ones to accompany Miss Elsie to New North Cemetery? We were kin. In 1827 Robert Calder had married Margaret "Peggy" Pinkham, one of the girls who grew up in the house at 12 Cliff Road. Peggy was the daughter of Captain Hezekiah Pinkham and sister of my great-great-grandmother Sarah Pinkham Bunker. Within a few years of her wedding, Peggy moved into a new home built by her husband at 10 Cliff Road, a stone's throw from her parents' house.

The house was splendid, but Peggy saw much sorrow there. Over a period of three years, three of the Calder children died. In grief she hadn't far to go to her parents and sister Sarah P. for solace. Ties between the two households remained strong even after Robert Jr. moved his family to Boston at the time of the Civil War. The Calder grandchildren were sent to spend the summers at 10 and 12 Cliff Road. When Sarah P. died, the Calders were given a grandfather clock from 12 Cliff Road in recognition of the enduring ties between her and Peggy.

In connection with her visit in 1952, Miss Elsie wrote to my mother, "Your mother, Hilda Gibbs, tells me that Robert Calder's house is now a rooming house. I plan to get a room there and contact your mother, as she can tell me the changes that have been made. Both my father and Uncle Eugene talk a great deal about Aunt Sarah. I think Maurice lived with her. She was a good cook."

Of the Calders, she wrote that they were all descendants of Scottish émigré Alexander Calder of Aberdeen, and of his son Samuel, who moved to Nantucket and married into the Coffin family. "Piece by piece," she wrote, "I am putting the Calder story together and enjoying it."

Grampa Gibbs could have told Miss Elsie about changes that had been made in the house at 10 Cliff Road after Robert and Peggy died in the early 1880s, but he had died thirty years before her visit. As for Hilda, she could hardly help, since Robert and Peggy had both died before Gram arrived in the U.S.A.

After their deaths, rights to the property passed to two cousins, and after one of them died, the surviving cousin sold the property to two other women. Several more transfers took place between 1944 and 1962, and at some point the Calders' house became a bed and breakfast establishment called the Century House. Throughout the summer of 1952, the year Elsie Calder visited the island, the Century House advertised in *Nantucket Holiday*, a newspaper supplement for vacationers.

The couple from Vermont who bought the house with all its contents in 1962 remained in business for twenty-two years. The foundation that bought it in 1984 appointed Jean Heron innkeeper, a position she has now held for more than a quarter of a century.

At that point, service as a guesthouse over so many decades had obliterated evidence of what the Calders' private home had been like in the 1800s. In 1910 a large veranda had been wrapped around the north and east sides of the building, providing a shady outdoor sitting room with rocking chairs. The interior had been divided into the maximum number of bedrooms. For Jean and her husband, Gerry Connick, there was no going back. Instead of attempting a historical restoration, they carried out a complete refurbishment of the house as a more elegant B&B with eighteen guest rooms, twenty-three baths, and a spacious open kitchen.

Their neighbors across the fence were Ellen Ramsdell and Esther Gibbs. Ever skeptical, Aunt Esther watched the work going on next door and issued frequent critical bulletins on the latest changes to the Calders' old house. The new owners gradually won her over, however, by dispatching workmen from their project to look after repairs and upkeep at 67 North Centre Street. By then Ellen, profoundly deaf and disabled, was housebound and confined to a wheelchair. Esther had all she could manage as Ellen's caregiver, and she accepted assistance from all quarters. She made friends with her newest neighbors about the same time she decided it was worthwhile to befriend my husband.

Jean and Gerry took over the Century House just after Al and I married. We have now been neighbors for many years. They frequently praise my efforts to return our gardens to something Ellen, the consummate horticulturist, would deem even minimally acceptable. When they are off-island in the winter, we help keep an eye on their property.

Whatever emerged from Peggy Calder's kitchen at 10 Cliff Road must have been very like what her sister Sarah P. prepared in the kitchen of 12 Cliff Road. When I was growing up nearby, we did not visit the proprietors of the Century House, nor did I so much as break bread with

Miss Elsie Calder. Until recently I had no culinary associations with the place or its people.

Times have changed. Jean and Gerry sent me the following essay about the bounteous breakfasts they serve to Century House guests—and sometimes to us, too.

> *At the time of the change of innkeepers, the basic staples of breakfast at the Century House were homemade doughnuts and coffee, placed outside in the lobby with no access for guests to the kitchen. When the present innkeepers reorganized the breakfast situation, they introduced breads and granolas along with fresh-perked coffee and afternoon chocolate chip cookies. The aromas of both entice people to leave their breezy rooms and set off for the beach in the morning or into town for the evening. As the years have gone by, the same basic recipes have been used for cereals and the breads. Coconut macaroons have been added along with cinnamon buns between breakfast and the afternoon cookies. The kitchen, along with the large veranda, is used to serve breakfast.*

Gerry has shared his recipe for the bread that is specially baked for the breakfasts served in the kitchen

CENTURY HOUSE BREAKFAST BREAD

Two loaves

The bread recipe that follows is basically a sourdough cinnamon-raisin-cranberry bread. Almost everyone likes cinnamon; combining it with raisins makes for a great aroma when toasted; and the cranberries are added to give an island flavor.

The bread recipe itself is a two- to three-day affair during which we make up a sour-dough starter. It has three parts, the starter, the soaker, and the biga.

The starter requires:
2 cups sponge (proof starter)
3 cups unbleached flour
2 tablespoons olive oil
4 teaspoons sugar
2 teaspoons salt
We mix it together and set it aside, following normal instructions for making a starter.

Along with that we make up the soaker. This is made up of:
1 1/3 cups whole wheat flour
3/8 teaspoon of salt
3/4 cup of soy milk
3/4 cup of raisins
3/4 cup of dried, sweetened cranberries
Combine the flour, salt, and milk and mix for a minute.
Add the raisins and cranberries, using wet hands to knead the dough until evenly mixed.
Cover loosely and refrigerate for a minimum of 24 hours. It should be good for up to three days. Remove from the refrigerator two hours before making the final dough.

The biga is made of:
1 1/3 cup whole wheat flour
1/4 teaspoon instant yeast
6 tablespoonsf soy milk
1/4 cup vegetable oil
1 large egg, slightly beaten.
Mix all ingredients together, letting the dough rest for 5 minutes.
Put the dough in a glass bowl, cover with plastic wrap, and refrigerate for at least 8 hours.
2 hours before making the final dough, remove from refrigerator.

The final dough is made up of the sourdough starter, the soaker, and the biga along with:
7 tablespoons whole wheat flour
5/8 teaspoon salt
2 1/4 teaspoons instant yeast
1 1/2 tablespoon honey
2 tablespoons brown sugar
1/2 teaspoon ground cinnamon
1/4 cup cinnamon sugar (3 tablespoons granulated sugar plus 2 teaspoons cinnamon).

Chop the soaker, the biga, and the sourdough starter into about a dozen small pieces each. (This makes it easier to work the three constituents together.) Sprinkle extra whole-wheat flour on the pieces to keep them from sticking to each other. Combine all the pieces in a large bowl with the 7 tablespoons of flour, salt, yeast, honey, and cinnamon.

Stir with a large spoon or knead with hands for two minutes until the dough is soft and slightly sticky. Add flour and water if needed.

Dust the work surface with flour, then roll the dough in the flour to coat. Form the dough into a ball and let it rest for five minutes while you prepare a clean bowl lightly oiled with vegetable oil.

Resume kneading the dough for one minute, form the dough into a ball and place into the bowl, rolling to coat with the oil. Cover loosely with plastic wrap and let it stand at room temperature for 45–60 minutes until it is 11/2 times its original size.

Dust the work surface with some extra flour and transfer the dough to the work surface. Roll the dough out to an 8-inch square about one half inch thick. Sprinkle cinnamon sugar over the surface and roll it up into two tight loaves. Place in 4 1/2 by 9-inch pans. Mist the top of the dough and cover loosely with plastic wrap.

Let rise at room temperature for 60 minutes until the loaf crests above the pan.

Pre-heat oven to 400°, lower temperature to 325° and bake for 20 minutes. Rotate the pans 180 degrees, and continue baking for another 25–40 minutes until the loaves are rich brown on all sides.

Transfer the loaves to a cooling rack and allow to cool an hour before serving.

Cinnamon rolls can be made in the same manner, rolling the dough out in thinner and narrower sheets and adding more cinnamon sugar to the top.

In conclusion, Gerry writes:

> *After reading this you can see why many people choose to stay at the Century House enjoying Nantucket's North Shore rather than staying home and spending three or four days making this bread.*

Gerry's instructions bring me back to standing next to Gram at her baking table, rolling out rectangles of dough, sprinkling them with cinnamon and sugar, and rolling them up—just as in his directions. His bread and cinnamon roll recipe is infinitely more complex than Gram's, but the principle remains the same. A North Shore culinary tradition carries on.

Jean E. Heron and Gerry Connick, innkeepers at the Century House

Epilogue

Excepting excursions to Finland, Texas, Mexico, and Hawaii, most of this memoir unfolds on one block, from 12 Cliff Road at the top of the hill to the North Shore Restaurant at the bottom of the hill, then halfway uphill again to 67 North Centre Street, concluding at 10 Cliff Road. It is gratifying and a little strange to end up just a half block from where I lived as a child, retracing my childhood footsteps every day and being reminded at every turn of the people who have lived here and the food they have brought to the table. Blessings upon them, each and every one.

The neighborhood viewed downhill from in front of 12 Cliff Road at the far right. In the center of the photo the North Church looms over the Cathcarts' North Shore grocery store. In the middle left is 67 N. Centre Street, and at the far left, the wrap-around veranda of the Century House at 10 Cliff Road.

This photo was taken after 1910, when the veranda was added to the Calder house but before the cobblestones were asphalted over in 1921.

Roberts House waitresses in uniform: Esther Gibbs at right

Appendix

Roberts House Menu for Thursday, July 29, 1937

Combination No. 1------75c

Scotch Broth or Chilled Pineapple Juice

Choice:

Pot Roast of Beef, Gravy

Baked Sausages, Bacon Strip

Fresh Swordfish, Tartar Sauce

Mashed Potatoes   Native Carrots
               Fresh String Beans

Hot Rolls   Butter

Choice of Desserts:

Homemade Apple Pie
Chocolate Layer Cake
Angel Cake a la Mode
Hot Fudge Sundae
Vanilla, Coffee Ice Cream

Coffee   Tea

Combination No. 2-----65c

Hot Vegetable Plate:

(Potatoes   Carrots   String Beans   Peas   Beets)

Hot Rolls   Butter

Hot Fudge Sundae or Coffee Jelly

Coffee   Tea

Sandwich Special------35c

Chopped Ham and Egg Sandwich

Coffee Jelly   Tea or Coffee

Pot of Tea (with Cream or Lemon) -----.15

Assorted [Homemade (crossed out)] Cookies ----- .10

Chocolate Layer Cake -----.15

Plain Ice Cream-----.10

Fudge Sundae-----.25

The North Shore Restaurant
80 Centre St.   Nantucket, Mass.

Recommended by:
A. L. A.
MOBILE GUIDE
WOMEN'S CITY CLUB OF BOSTON
Member of Nantucket Chamber of Commerce

Esther U. Gibbs
OWNER – MANAGER

In the early days of Nantucket, the section of the town where the NORTH SHORE RESTAURANT is located was called "North Shore."

The restaurant is located on the site where Benjamin Franklin's grandfather's mill stood. Along here was once an opening to the sea known as BARZILLAI'S CREEK, which was broad enough to sail boats to GULL ISLAND. Nowadays the approach to the house known as Gull Island is from a lane that leads off to the left, just beyond the restaurant.

The LILY POND once surrounded Gull Island, and there was an earthen dam to control the water until a little girl, LOVE SWAIN, on her way home from play with a shell or stick in her hand, made a small hole in the dam and let the water out. She told no one but went to bed early to be awakened by her father's voice saying that someone had let the water out of the Lily Pond and all the boats in the Creek had gone out to sea.

The little girl never told anyone what had happened until, in her eighties, she called a few people around her while she lay on her death bed and confessed the story as told above.

After the pond was drained, and there was no water to run the mill, the land was filled in, and a grocery store was built and operated by various owners and called NORTH SHORE GROCERY. In 1943, I purchased the building and converted it into a restaurant. While digging the cellar I found the base of the old mill and brick drains.

The dining room is decorated in the era of whaling days with authentic relics, many of which were in my family; others I have obtained.

At breakfast you may help yourself to a cup of coffee to drink while waiting for your breakfast to be served.

A different menu is prepared daily of home-cooked food specializing in Quahaug Chowder, Garlic Shrimp, Fish in season, Steaks, Chops, and a variety of home-made breads and pastries at moderate prices.

I have had many compliments on the cleanliness of my kitchen.

Esther U. Gibbs
Owner–Manager

Contents of memorandum book: North Shore Restaurant, 1958

Monday–Saturday:

Breakfast	7:45	-	11:15
Dinner	5:00	-	9:30

Sunday:

Breakfast	8:30	-	12:20
Dinner	5:00	-	9.00

Fowl

Roast chicken	1.90
Roast turkey	1.90
Chicken pie	1.75
Chicken à la king	1.85
Roast duckling	2.30
1/2 broiled chicken	1.85
Chicken croquettes	1.55
Duck Oriental	
Rock Cornish game hen	3.10
Creamed chicken	
Coq au vin	
1/4 chicken, fried or oven baked, with cream gravy	1.85
Chicken salad, french fries, rolls	
Chicken Cacciatore	1.85
Chicken Tetrazzini	1.85

Beef

Broiled filet mignon (on special)	4.50
Tenderloin Stroganoff	2.75
Beef Stroganoff	2.50
Minute steak	
Hash	1.60
Swedish meatballs	1.70
Calves liver and bacon	1.95
Pot roast	1.95
Meatloaf	1.65
Roast ribs	2.55
Braised beef	1.85
Tenderloin	3.50
Boneless sirloin	3.50
Filet mignon	
Veal cutlet	1.90
Beef steak pie	1.85
Beef casserole	1.85
Round steak	
Broiled minute sirloin	2.50
Broiled tenderloin	
Veal Parmigiana	1.90
Veal Scallopine	

Lamb

Lamb chops	2.10 – 3.00
Smaller chops, order separate	2.55
Roast lamb	1.95
Lamb casserole	1.80
Shepherd's pie	1.65
Braised lamb & rice	1.75
Shoulder lamb chop	1.95

Pork

Baked ham	
Pork chops	1.75 (1)
	2.25 (2)
Grilled ham	1.95
Broiled ham	1.95
Roast pork	1.90
Spare ribs	
Minced ham on toast	
Ham croquettes	1.65

Seafood

Baked stuffed lobster	3.25
Lobster Newburg	2.95
Lobster salad	2.95
Lobster croquettes	1.95

Lobster Thermidor	2.95
Lobster sauté	2.95
Fried butterfly shrimp	2.25
Broiled garlic shrimp	2.85
Fried bay scallops	
Broiled bay scallops	
Fried deep sea scallops	1.85
Broiled deep sea scallops	
Devilled crab	2.00
Frogs legs	
Soft shelled crabs	2.00
Quahaug pie	
Seafood platter	1.95
with lobster	2.25
Fillet of sole	1.85
Broiled bluefish	2.00
Plaicefish	1.85
Broiled salmon	1.90
Broiled swordfish	2.00
Mackerel	1.65
Halibut	1.85
Haddock	1.85
Broiled codfish	1.70
Bass	2.00
Fried clams	2.00
Salmon salad	1.75
Escalloped bass, cod, salmon, or sole	1.65
Escalloped swordfish	1.65

Scallop stew (cup)

Marinated herring

Lobster bisque   .50

Quahaug chowder   . 35 – small

                                              .70 - large

Salad   .25

Rolls & butter   .15

Side order beans   .35

Order french fries   .25

Vegetable plate   1.35

Side dish vegetables   .25

Misc.

Beans   1.35

Beans and ham   1.70

Beans and fish cakes   1.60

Stuffed pepper   1.60

Hash   1.60

Hot roast beef sandwich   1.65

Spaghetti & meatballs

Tomato with crabmeat

New England Boiled Dinner   2.65

New England Boiled Dinner as a special   1.90

Desserts

Strawberry ice cream cake	.35
Ice cream cake with chocolate sauce	.35
Angel cake with frozen strawberries	.35
Angel cake with fresh strawberries	.40
Angel cake with chocolate sauce	.30
Individual angel cake with strawberries	.35
Peach shortcake with canned peaches	.35
Peach shortcake with fresh peaches	.40
Fresh strawberry shortcake	.45
Frozen strawberry shortcake	.40
Baba au rhum	.40
Fresh fruit cup	.35
Chowder	.35 (small)
	.70 (large)
Soups	.25

Patio Service

Broiled or grilled minute sirloin	2.00
Grilled minute steak	1.50
Grilled ham steak	1.65
Chicken a la King	1.50
Hamburg Stroganoff	1.00
Chopped sirloin	1.25
Roast beef hash	1.25
Cold cuts	1.25
1/2 cold boiled lobster	1.75
Sautéed lobster, petitpois, salad	2.50
Tenderloin steak sandwich	1.35
Tomato stuffed with lobster	1.85
Hot roast beef sandwich, mashed potatoes, peas	1.50
Tomato stuffed with crabmeat	1.50
Cold ham, potato salad, nut bread	1.25
1/2 broiled chicken, petit pois, hot reg. bread	1.50
Tomato stuffed with tuna	.95
Chop Suey with rice	.95
Cold corned beef & potato salad	1.25
Tomato stuffed with chicken salad	1.50
Cold boiled lobster, potato chips, tomato salad	2.95
Meatloaf, tomatoes, vegetables, chips	1.25

Lobster Bisque	small .50
	large .95

Sandwiches:

Cream Cheese & olive	.45
Nut Bread & Cream Cheese	.45
Tuna fish	.60
Sliced chicken	.85
Crabmeat salad	.85
Ham salad	.65
Cold corned beef	.65
Ham salad	.65
Club	1.25
Sandwich loaf	.65
Tuna fish roll	.85
Chicken salad roll	.85
Crabmeat roll	.85
Lobster roll	.85

Salad Plates:

Tuna salad with nut bread	1.15
Chicken salad with nut bread	1.50
Fresh lobster salad with nut bread	2.25
Tuna salad bowl	1.15

Garden Gate Price List

PRODUCTS FROM

Ellen L. Ramsdell's

Garden Gate

Nantucket Island

Mass.

All are home made in small quantities, never any artificial pectin used. Only the best grade of imported spices used in my preserves and relishes.

JELLIES, JAMS, MARMALADES

Nantucket Spiced Cranberry	85¢
Nantucket Whole Cranberry Sauce	75¢
Nantucket Cranberry Jelly	75¢
Nantucket Wild Beach Plum Jelly	75¢
Nantucket Wild Beach Plum Jam	75¢
Nantucket Wild Grape Jelly	75¢

Nantucket Wild Grape Jam	75¢
Nantucket Blackberry Jam	75¢
Nantucket Rose Hip Jam	75¢
Peach Jam	75¢
Heavenly Jam	75¢
Pineapple Apricot Jam	75¢
Orange Marmalade	75¢
Cranberry Apple Jam	75¢
Cranberry Conserve	85¢
Cranberry Orange Relish	75¢
Six Fruit Marmalade	85¢

RELISHES

Sweet Pepper Relish	85¢
Chili Sauce	75¢
Piccalilli	75¢
Watermelon Rind Pickle	85¢
Citron Rind Pickle	85¢
Gooseberry Relish (hot)	85¢
Nantucket Cranberry and Pineapple Chutney	85¢

Please do not ask to ship **less than 6 jars**.

Parcel Post charges are extra.

Any assortment of your choice.

Mincemeat made from an old Nantucket recipe:

Pints	**$1.25**
Quarts:	**$2.25**

Also:

Home Made Fudge & Penuche $1.60 lb.

Christmas orders packed with native greens and berries.

Ellen Ramsdell and the Garden Gate gift shop

The Century House brochure

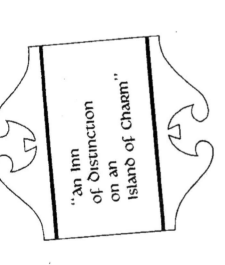

the Century house motto
for 100 years

"an Inn
of Distinction
on an
Island of Charm"

The Century House is located in the residential section of the Old Historic District on prestigious Cliff Road. From here, it is but a short walk to Jetties Beach, Steamboat Wharf and Main Street.

Most of our rooms have private bathrooms and six rooms enjoy the charm of old fireplaces. Each room features its own distinctive and unique picturesque view of historic Nantucket. The nineteenth century parlor is the visual and social focal point of the inn. The overall decor is authentically typical of the lovely Laura Ashley style.

A complimentary continental breakfast is included with all rooms.

This gracious home was constructed in 1833 in the Late Federal style and features a handsome veranda along its frontage. Guests are intrigued by the Nantucket County ambience and, more importantly, by our old fashioned hospitality and service.

In addition to the main house, we also have a separate guest cottage with its own kitchen facilities. This rustic building of post and beam construction was moved to its present location during the Civil War and served as a blacksmith shop into the early 1900's. Perfect for a couple or small family.

Across the island at 'Sconset Beach, a second cottage is available. This lovely rose-covered sanctuary from the mainland is just 200 yards from the ocean and oozes charm both within and without. It is an ideal hideaway for the romantic couple of any age! Includes kitchen facilities, a kingsize bed and Jacuzzi.

Innkeepers: Jean E. Heron   Gerry Connick

Culinary Index

Index of Recipes

About the Author

Frances Ruley Karttunen was born in Boston in 1942 and brought home to Nantucket at ten days old aboard the SS *Nobska*. She had an academic career in linguistics based at the University of Texas at Austin. Since 2000 she has lived year-round on Nantucket, devoting herself to writing local history, especially the dynamics between the "descended Nantucketers" typified by her Nantucket grandfather and his family and the people she refers to as "the other islanders," including her immigrant grandmother. More than a simple fusion of New England and Scandinavian cookery, she sees her home cuisine as an expression of Nantucketers' historic cosmopolitanism and global curiosity.

Made in the USA
Charleston, SC
24 April 2011